Communications

Other Publications:
SUCCESSFUL PARENTING
HEALTHY HOME COOKING
YOUR HOME
THE ENCHANTED WORLD
THE KODAK LIBRARY OF CREATIVE PHOTOGRAPHY
GREAT MEALS IN MINUTES
THE CIVIL WAR
PLANET EARTH
COLLECTOR'S LIBRARY OF THE CIVIL WAR
THE EPIC OF FLIGHT
THE GOOD COOK
WORLD WAR II
HOME REPAIR AND IMPROVEMENT
THE OLD WEST

This volume is one of a series that examines
various aspects of computer technology and the
role computers play in modern life.

UNDERSTANDING COMPUTERS

Communications

BY THE EDITORS OF TIME-LIFE BOOKS

TIME-LIFE BOOKS, ALEXANDRIA, VIRGINIA

Contents

The Glimmer of Electronic Connections

During the mid-1980s, a new craze seized Paris and much of France. Every day, hundreds of thousands of French telephone customers, in homes and offices, sat down at a chic computer terminal called Le Minitel and went "on-line." Typing various combinations of letters and numbers, they summoned to the terminal's nine-inch black-and-white screen a stream of text and images representing an astonishing array of services and information. Through the Minitel, for example, they could check a bank credit-card balance, buy a suit or dress, scan the morning newspaper, read the latest weather report or leave a message in a friend's electronic mailbox.

More popular than any of these activities was one called Dialog. Though the words were typed rather than spoken into the machines, Dialog often resembled a telecommunications free-for-all, in which anyone who wished to could join a conversation. Flirtatious participants adopted pseudonyms that freed them to spice their repartee with sexual innuendo. Dialog and other services expanded so rapidly that several times during the summer of 1985 the volume of subscribers attempting to use their terminals overloaded the system's main computer. Like a power grid sapped by too many air conditioners turned on in steamy weather, the computer shut down, leaving Minitel addicts to sweat it out until service could be restored.

This remarkable system of computer communications is called Teletel. Launched in 1981 by the government-owned telephone and postal monopoly, Postes, Télécommunications et Télédiffusion (P.T.T.)., Teletel was conceived mainly as an electronic telephone directory. P.T.T. officials expected the service to pay for itself by reducing both the number of telephone books printed and the need for directory-assistance operators. Private companies soon began to offer banking, entertainment and information services on the system, drawn by the promise of revenues amounting to 60 percent of the fees paid by Teletel customers to P.T.T. By 1986, the number of on-line services exceeded 2,000, having increased tenfold in just one year.

Teletel is not inexpensive. Home subscribers to the service pay nothing for the terminal, but they are charged for connect time — the period they are dialed into Teletel — at the rate of about 13 cents per minute. At such prices, it is easy to run up a substantial Teletel bill, as one Parisian marketing executive discovered. In a single month, his mildly insomniac 17-year-old daughter spent 500 francs — some $65 — just playing games available on the network.

Teletel has proved to be much more than a break-even proposition, earning about $70 million a year for P.T.T. According to Daniel P. Resnick, a history professor at Pittsburgh's Carnegie-Mellon University and former executive director of a French government agency established to encourage the use of computers, Teletel "is an enormous public success, the most promising public experiment using telephone lines in the world, and the audience is unlimited."

Granted, the future of an infant such as Teletel is always difficult to predict. And telecomputing, a word coined to describe the computer's impact on telecommunications, has had its share of unfulfilled promises. But there is little doubt that a revolution is under way, leading to the day when — as John F. Akers, the president of IBM, has put it — "everything is connected to everything."

A LONG-STANDING DESIRE

Ages before there was anything remotely resembling Teletel, the human need for connection was clear. People went to enormous lengths to share news or warn one another of danger when the unaided human voice was an inadequate medium. They devised intricate drum codes that carried through the densest jungle, smoke signals that puffed from hilltops to be scanned by watchers miles away, semaphore flags whose codes could be deciphered across a span of water between ships. Today, drums and bonfires have given way to electronic pulses, but as the Teletel phenomenon demonstrates, the driving force is the same: to send messages, make connections, communicate. By way of regular telephone links, private cables snaking through the hidden spaces of a building and microwave radio transmissions relayed by communications satellites or by land-based repeater stations, electronic signals zip back and forth for innumerable purposes. Billions of dollars are transferred between banks and across oceans; on a smaller scale, computerized teller machines disburse $20 bills to a bank's customers, relieving human tellers of routine transactions. Telecomputing can automate production in an entire manufacturing facility or permit desktop computers to share software or a central repository of information.

Communications between computers have become extraordinarily fast. When the first long-distance communications link between a computing machine and a remote terminal was established almost five decades ago, information in the form of binary digits, or bits, was transmitted at the rate of fewer than 50 bits per second. With modern satellites and fiber-optics technology — the art of communicating with light pulsed along fine filaments of glass — data may fly between distant computers at 1.5 million bits per second — a speed that would allow Herman Melville's 222,000-word masterpiece *Moby Dick* to be sent from one computer to another in less than 30 seconds.

Since the beginning of computer communications, the vast majority of computer data has traveled along ordinary telephone circuits, the ubiquitous network that makes it possible for anyone with a telephone to speak with virtually anyone else on earth who also possesses such an instrument. But the union of computers and the phone network was an unnatural one. Telephone circuits were designed to handle the electrical equivalent, or analog, of the human voice. The telephone converts a speaker's words into an electrical voltage whose frequency varies according to the pitch of the voice and whose amplitude increases or decreases according to its loudness *(pages 30-31)*. Computers, in contrast, express information in digital form, as a stream of discrete electrical pulses.

This incompatibility between computer data and the telephone network was resolved by a clever translating device called a modem (from modulator-demodulator). Inserted between a computer and the phone system at the origin of a transmission, it converts, or modulates, the computer's digital output into analog signals, which can be handled like a telephone call. At the receiving end, the modem demodulates the incoming telephone signal, restoring the information to the digital form acceptable to the computer.

For many, the modem has been associated exclusively with computers, especially the desktop variety. Yet in the fast-paced context of electrical communications, the modem is practically as ancient as the wheel. Its origins can be traced to the merging of devices invented for similar purposes but fundamentally different in their technology — the telegraph, the telephone and the teletypewriter.

The telegraph preceded the telephone by more than 30 years and the teletypewriter by half a century, and in some ways it was the forerunner of telecomputing. To begin with, the telegraph, like the modern computer, was a digital medium. Depressing the sending key sent a discrete pulse of electricity along an iron wire to a distant destination. The transmission had three states: off, on for a short time (a dot) and on for a longer time (a dash).

Speed of transmission was an important consideration from the outset. Adopting the dot-and-dash system made it possible for telegraphy's inventor, Samuel F. B. Morse, and his assistant, Alfred Vail, to represent the alphabet and numbers with far fewer keystrokes than a two-state system would have permitted. To reduce to the minimum the time it would take to transmit a message, Morse and Vail decided that the most frequently used letters of the alphabet would be indicated by the shortest possible sequences of dots and dashes. They visited a printer and counted the pieces of type in each letter case; e's and t's outnumbered all other letters, reflecting the frequent appearance of the pair in the English language. So Morse and Vail represented the letter e with a single dot and the letter t with a single dash. This rational approach resulted in a telegraphic code that could send messages at the rate of about two characters — equivalent to the now-modest rate of 15 bits — per second.

In 1844, with the aid of a congressional appropriation of $30,000, Morse inaugurated long-distance telegraph service in the United States. From Washington, D.C., he tapped out the dots and dashes signifying the Biblical text, "What hath God wrought!" The electric pulses sped along 37 miles of wire to Baltimore, Maryland, where Vail received the staccato stream of pulses and repeated it back to Washington. Seventeen years later, the telegraph spanned the continent, replacing the fabled Pony Express, which had previously relayed messages through 157 stations along the 1,840-mile route between St. Joseph, Missouri, and San Francisco.

TELEGRAPHY GOES BINARY
A telegraphic technology that would more directly influence the development of computers and telecomputing arrived with the advent of teletypewriting machines. Depressing one of the typewriter-like keys on a teletypewriter transmitted a two-state code of on-off pulses rather than the three-state code used by Morse. In the Baudot code — employed by practically all teletypewriters and named for 19th-century French telegrapher Émile Baudot, who invented it — each character on the keyboard was represented by a unique combination of five on-or-off signals, or bits. Five bits can be combined in only 32 ways, however — not

Mapping the Frequency Spectrum

Whatever the medium or type of message — telegram, phone conversation, television program or computer data — modern communications depend on manipulating and controlling signals within the electromagnetic spectrum. Electromagnetic signals are wavelike oscillations that can be described in terms of either length (the distance between the peaks of two waves) or frequency (the number of wave cycles per second, expressed as hertz): the shorter the wavelength, the higher the frequency. The spectrum ranges from extremely low-frequency radio waves of 30 hertz — with a wavelength of nearly the earth's diameter — to high-frequency cosmic rays of more than 10 million trillion hertz, with wavelengths smaller than the nucleus of an atom.

Because of its extraordinary breadth, the electromagnetic spectrum is depicted below as a logarithmic progression: The scale increases by multiples of 10, so that its higher regions encompass a greater span of frequencies than the lower regions. For example, the range of visible light, while appearing rather narrow in the upper-middle part of the scale, embraces nearly 400 trillion hertz, or approximately 4,000 times the frequency range (and potential information-carrying capacity) of radio signals at the lower end of the scale shown here.

The range of frequencies making up a signal is called a bandwidth. The human voice, for example, can typically generate frequencies from 100 to 10,000 hertz, for a bandwidth of 9,900 hertz; laser optical fibers, in contrast, operate over a band of 200 trillion hertz. Because the ear does not require a vast range of frequencies to elicit meaning from ordinary speech, the phone company typically allots a total bandwidth of 4,000 hertz for voice transmis-

sion (below). The wide bands of fiber optics and other high-frequency media, such as microwaves, can thus accommodate many phone conversations, once the signal has been translated to a higher frequency.

The various transmission media shown below effectively span the electromagnetic spectrum, from radio waves through visible light. Twisted-pair wires, typically used in local telephone networks, transmit relatively low frequencies compared with the coaxial cables used for long-distance phone lines, cable television and high-capacity local data networks. By international agreement, the radio segment of the electromagnetic spectrum is divided into numerous bands that are allocated (on a different basis in different parts of the world) to such applications as TV broadcast, citizens-band radio or marine communications.

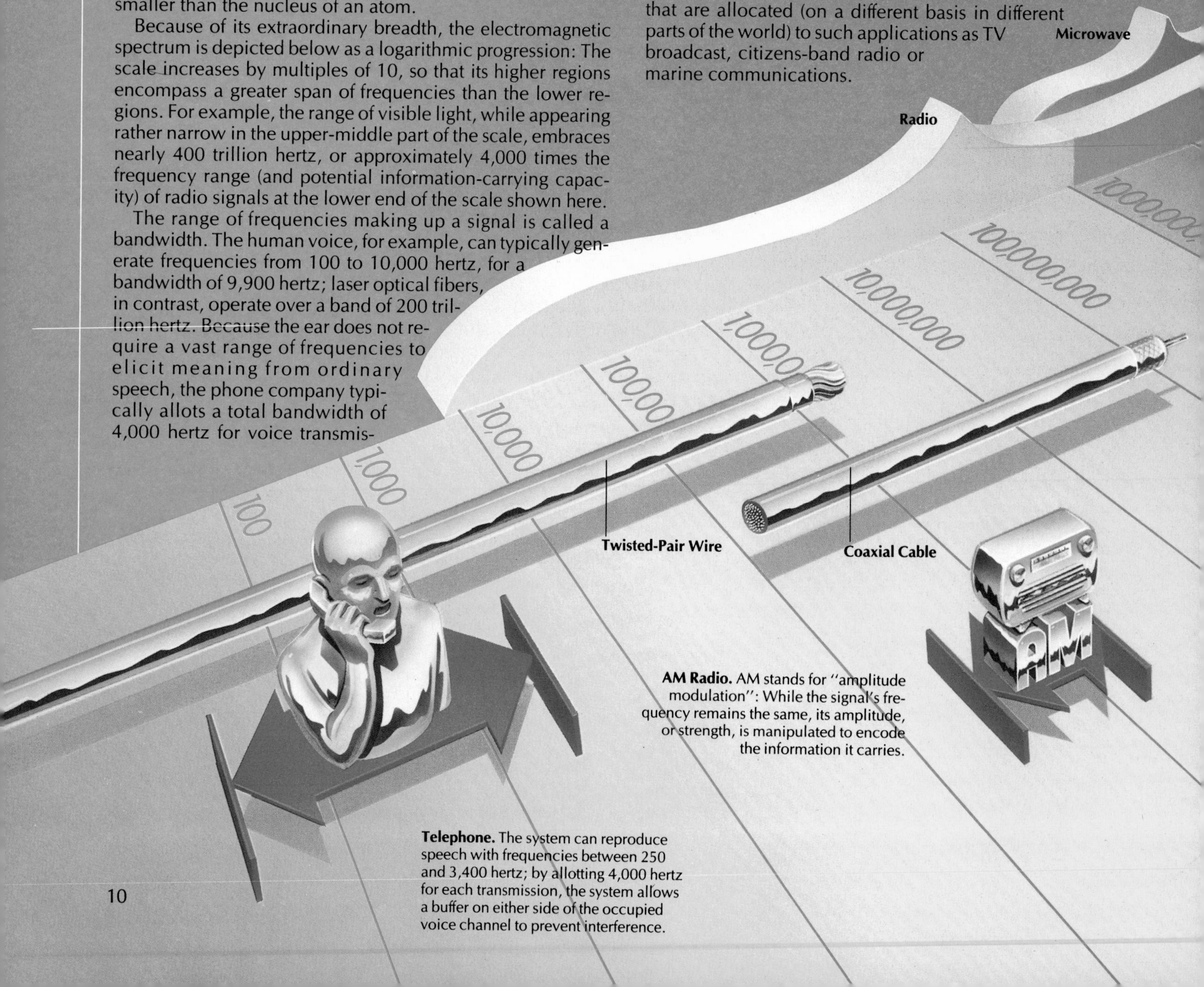

Microwave

Radio

Twisted-Pair Wire

Coaxial Cable

AM Radio. AM stands for "amplitude modulation": While the signal's frequency remains the same, its amplitude, or strength, is manipulated to encode the information it carries.

Telephone. The system can reproduce speech with frequencies between 250 and 3,400 hertz; by allotting 4,000 hertz for each transmission, the system allows a buffer on either side of the occupied voice channel to prevent interference.

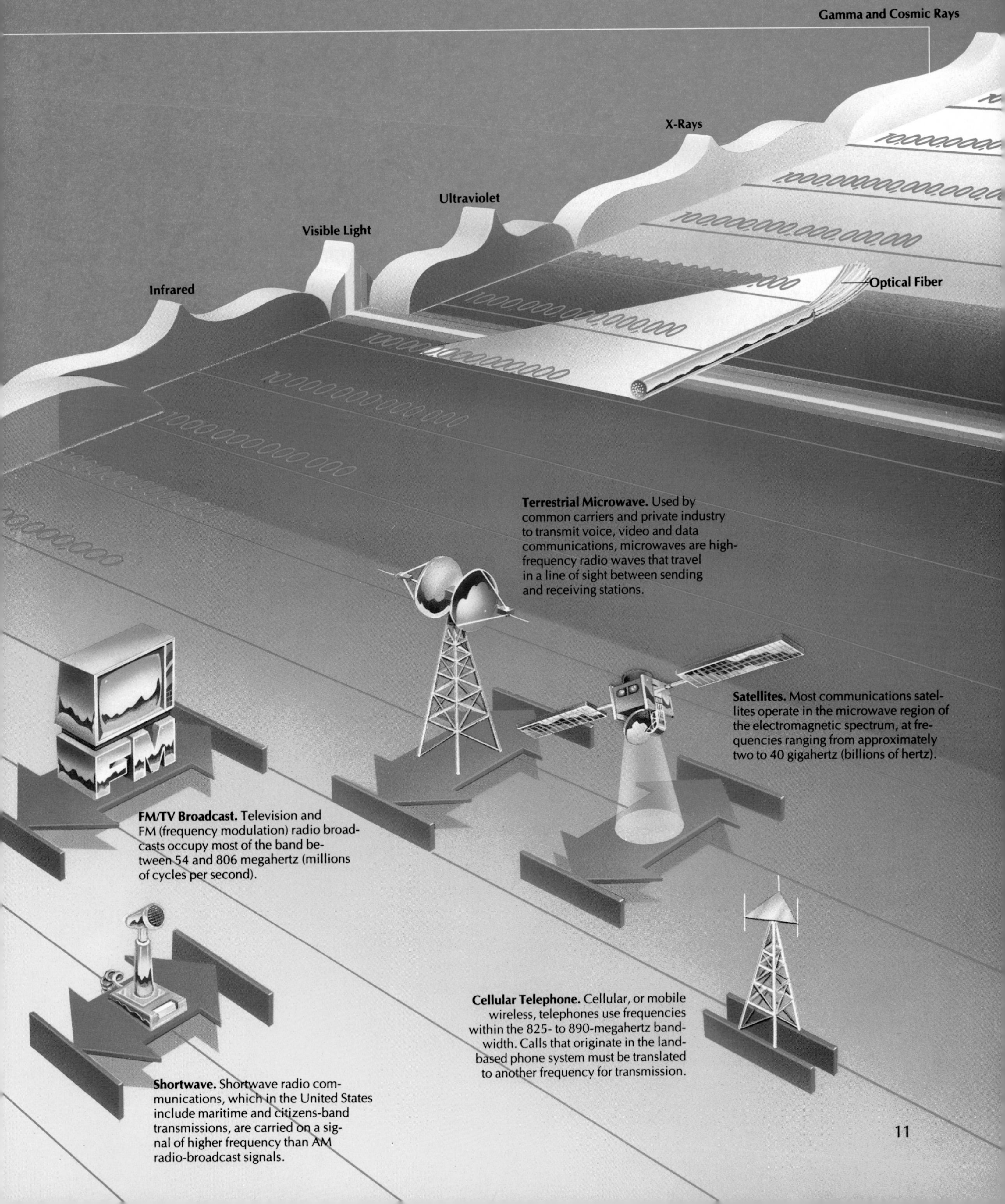

Gamma and Cosmic Rays

X-Rays

Ultraviolet

Visible Light

Infrared

Optical Fiber

Terrestrial Microwave. Used by common carriers and private industry to transmit voice, video and data communications, microwaves are high-frequency radio waves that travel in a line of sight between sending and receiving stations.

Satellites. Most communications satellites operate in the microwave region of the electromagnetic spectrum, at frequencies ranging from approximately two to 40 gigahertz (billions of hertz).

FM/TV Broadcast. Television and FM (frequency modulation) radio broadcasts occupy most of the band between 54 and 806 megahertz (millions of cycles per second).

Cellular Telephone. Cellular, or mobile wireless, telephones use frequencies within the 825- to 890-megahertz bandwidth. Calls that originate in the land-based phone system must be translated to another frequency for transmission.

Shortwave. Shortwave radio communications, which in the United States include maritime and citizens-band transmissions, are carried on a signal of higher frequency than AM radio-broadcast signals.

11

enough to encode the alphabet and the numerals zero through nine as well as punctuation marks and necessary control characters, such as the space and the carriage return. Baudot's solution was, in effect, to double the number of combinations by using two of the 32 keys to shift between two sets of meanings for the remaining 30. The transmission of one of the shift codes signaled that subsequent characters would be letters and other so-called lower-case characters; the other shift code switched the machine to characters such as numerals and punctuation, which were designated upper case.

One of the earliest teletypewriters was invented during the late 1890s by Donald Murray, a New Zealander. Murray was working at a newspaper in Sydney, Australia, at the time, and he originally intended his machine as an automatic typesetter. When little came of that endeavor, he applied the same principle to telegraphy. The heart of Murray's teletypewriter was a rotating drum. When the operator pressed a key, a complex chain of mechanical and electrical events began, culminating in the transmission of a letter.

In its early form, Murray's teletypewriter was so crudely built that *Scientific American* magazine likened it to "a sort of cross between a sewing machine and a barrel organ." Because the drum had to be turned manually by a wooden handle, skeptics called it "Murray's coffee mill" or "the Australian sausage machine." But Murray improved the machine—first in the U.S., and then in England with the backing of the British post office—by adding, among other features, an electric motor to turn the drum; he put his device into service in 1903. Teletypes, as they came to be called, required far less training and skill than the Morse telegraph. Anyone who could type now qualified as a telegrapher.

THE SPEED OF PAPER TAPE

As teletype machines evolved, they gained the capability of transmitting in two different modes. In the direct mode, typing on the keyboard of one machine sent Baudot-coded signals through wires to trigger printing of the message by a similar machine at the other end. In the indirect mode, the act of typing caused the signals to be translated into rows of holes punched in a narrow strip of paper tape, with each row of possible holes representing one character. The presence or absence of a hole signaled on or off—or in the binary system, the digits one or zero. Next, the punched tape was fed through an automatic transmitter that generated electrical impulses corresponding to the presence or absence of holes, sending the signals along to perforate a similar tape at the other end. This tape then was put through a reader that caused the teletype to print out the message. By transmitting with tape instead of directly from the keyboard, where speed was limited by typing skills, operators could send up to about 60 bits per second, or 75 words per minute. Furthermore, the taped message could be forwarded by the automatic transmitter at the convenience of the sender or receiver, freeing them of the obligation to be present at their terminals simultaneously.

Clattering away in their five-bit Baudot, teletypes blazed many trails later followed by the computer. Paper-tape readers and punches, for example, were essential to many early computers, and telegrams were actually the first electronic mail. Teletype networks also handled airline reservations and served as information services, providing up-to-the-moment weather data and stock-market quotations. They acted as a communications tool for big corporations and, during World War II, for U.S. President Franklin D. Roosevelt and British Prime Minister Winston Churchill, who wished to "chat" across the Atlantic and have a written record of their conversations. Teletypes allowed department stores to swap credit information and banks to transfer funds. They furnished a kind of electronic bulletin board for police agencies, linking them from coast to coast and printing information on stolen vehicles and fugitive criminals. They transmitted news from around the world to local newspapers and even fulfilled Donald Murray's turn-of-the-century dream by perforating tape that, when fed to Linotype machines, automatically set the news in type.

BELL'S MARVELOUS INVENTION

For all its advances, telegraphy has remained an impersonal medium of communication. Messages bear no signature. And a truly conversational exchange of views on a subject is for all practical purposes impossible. From telegraphy's earliest days, shortcomings such as these had intensified the search for a way that one person might speak with another at greater than shouting distance.

The solution, of course, was the telephone. When Alexander Graham Bell constructed the device in 1876, he was actually attempting to create a harmonic telegraph. This apparatus was to permit several telegraph messages to be transmitted at the same time over one wire, saving the expense of stringing multiple telegraph lines to accommodate traffic on busy routes. Bell's idea was to have many sending keys in a telegraph office connected to a single circuit; the keys would send dots and dashes at different frequencies, or pitches, instead of identical ones that, if mixed together, would be impossible to resolve into the original messages. Receivers at the destination, each responding to a different frequency, would untangle the jumble of messages. In practice, the system was unreliable, but the principle worked well enough to convince Bell that many frequencies — even as many as produced by the human voice — could be sent simultaneously over a single wire.

The telephone soon gained popularity, spreading through communities large and small, and ultimately extending across the nation. Western Union, principal provider of telegraph service in the U.S., benefited enormously from the expansion of the telephone network. By 1888, when the first intercity telephone circuits were established, it was possible to send telegraph messages and telephone conversations at the same time over the same wires by employing an early version of a process known as frequency-division multiplexing *(pages 32-33)*. Because voice messages contain little sound below about 250 hertz, or cycles per second, the band of frequencies from that point down to zero hertz went unused in the phone system. Inasmuch as a telegrapher of superior skills could transmit only about 30 words per minute — the equivalent of 20 hertz — there was a gap of more than 200 hertz between the top of the telegraph's bandwidth, or possible range of frequencies *(pages 10-11)*, and the bottom of the voice bandwidth.

With such ample separation between the signals, even the comparatively crude, frequency-sensitive filters that were available around the turn of the century could easily separate a telegraph message from a voice message traveling the same wire. Thus the analog voice waves of a telephone conversation could travel in the bandwidth between 250 hertz and 3,400 hertz, while the digital pulses of telegraphy streamed along in the lower band. As a result, Western Union was able to establish telegraph connections anywhere that a telephone line went. Though fees were paid to the Bell Company for use of the lines, Western Union was spared the expense of stringing its own wires.

Frequency-division multiplexing was greatly enhanced during the 1920s when the telephone system "went electronic," in the words of one historian. The newly perfected vacuum tube permitted Bell engineers to devise a way to transmit multiple telephone conversations on a single circuit. They accomplished this by boosting the 250- to 3,400-hertz frequency band of a voice on the telephone up to higher frequency ranges — 4,250 to 7,650 hertz, 8,250 to 11,650 hertz, and so on — before transmission between telephone exchanges. At the telephone exchange near the destination, the signals were restored to the original frequency band and then routed to the recipient. Improved filters and a gap of 600 hertz between adjacent voice frequency bands prevented transmissions from contaminating one another. By this process, up to a dozen conversations could travel simultaneously on one circuit.

Analogous techniques were then applied to both telegraph and teletype messages, making those transmissions indistinguishable from a voice message as far as the telephone network was concerned. This piggybacking on the telephone system was particularly significant to the growth of teletyping because telephone lines went into the offices of business and government, where teletypes soon found widespread application.

At first the equipment that modulated and demodulated the teletype signals consisted of bulky, vacuum-tube circuitry located at the telephone company's central offices. By the late 1950s, as the demand for computer-to-computer communication began to increase, the electronics had acquired the name "modem" and were built into the terminals — which bore an external resemblance to the teletypewriter — used with computers of the day.

LONG-DISTANCE DATA

In 1940, nearly two decades before there was any such thing as a modem, the first long-distance transmission of computer signals took place. The central figure in the event was George R. Stibitz, a young mathematician at Bell Telephone Laboratories, the research arm of AT&T. Stibitz, an experimenter at heart, had been intrigued by electrical gadgets since childhood, an interest that on occasion must have dismayed his parents. As a boy of eight in Dayton, Ohio, he nearly set the house on fire by overloading the circuits with an electric motor given him by his father, a professor of theology.

But Stibitz' penchant for tinkering eventually led to several notable landmarks in computing. In 1937, Stibitz put together in his spare time the first machine developed in the U.S. to do binary arithmetic. Stibitz built the prototype at home, wiring together telephone-system components, batteries and other parts into the device, which he called the Model K — because he assembled it on the kitchen table. Then, in collaboration with Samuel B. Williams, a veteran Bell engineer who specialized in the switching equipment and techniques used in telephone networking, Stibitz developed a more ambitious machine — a digital calculator designed to handle complex numbers, a class of mathematical entities encountered in the design of long-distance telephone networks and elsewhere.

The resulting machine, which Stibitz called the Complex Number Calculator, was one of the earliest digital computers. It became operational early in 1940 at Bell Labs' Manhattan headquarters. Input and output for the machine were accommodated by a keyboard and printer adapted from standard teletype equipment. The calculator, which was locked in a closet, was soon linked to three of the teletype terminals, each located on a different floor of the building.

The Complex Number Calculator drew the attention of the American Mathematical Society, which invited Stibitz to present a paper on the machine to a meeting at Dartmouth College in Hanover, New Hampshire. To show off the computer's prowess, Dr. T. C. Fry, Stibitz' boss, suggested that he take numerical problems from the audience and telephone them to a keyboard operator in New York for solution. But Stibitz had a better idea. "With my usual genius for making things more difficult for myself and others," he wrote later, "I suggested direct telegraph operation from Hanover, and this was decided upon."

In New York, the three terminals communicated with the Stibitz computer over several wires—one for each number, mathematical sign and control character—bundled inside a cable. Running a cable the 250 miles from Hanover to New York was out of the question but, Stibitz suggested, an ordinary teletype circuit would serve the purpose.

Stibitz' collaborator, Sam Williams, went to work. Williams, whom Stibitz remembered later as "a quiet, very hard worker who seldom got very excited," built a special terminal that would encode each keystroke for transmission over the Bell system's Teletypewriter Exchange (TWX) service. The system he devised was a modification of the teletype's standard Baudot code. A decoder at the receiving end in New York restored the signals to the form required to operate the calculator. Furthermore, to avoid overloading the calculator, Williams designed the terminal to lock the keyboard momentarily after each keystroke. A fraction of a second later, after the calculator in New York signaled that the instruction had arrived, the keyboard unlocked to accept the next part of the problem.

On September 11, 1940, Stibitz staged his demonstration of long-distance computing as part of his presentation at Dartmouth. In the audience were three men in particular who would exert a profound influence on computer science: mathematicians John von Neumann and Norbert Wiener, and John W. Mauchly, who a few years later helped invent ENIAC, the world's first large-scale electronic digital computer. Stibitz, Wiener and others typed in complex-number problems on the keyboard, and within a minute the correct answer to each problem came racing back across the wire from the computer in New York.

THE QUEST FOR SPEED BEGINS

Williams' scheme for transmitting digital data to a computer was notably unhurried, loafing along at less than teletype speed. But transmission speed was not a critical factor at the time: An electromechanical calculator such as Stibitz' took almost a minute to answer an arithmetic problem that would occupy a modern computer for no more than a few ten-thousandths of a second. When modems came along for teletypewriters, some were capable of transmitting at the rate of 300 bits per second, more than fast enough for machines that were mechanically

15

The Itinerary of a Telephone Call

Physically connecting each of the world's 600 million telephones directly to every other phone would make a chaotic tangle of transmission lines, even if enough lines could be supplied. Instead, all telephones — and increasingly, computers — are attached to a communications network that establishes temporary connections. Computer-controlled facilities, called switches, shift a call from one path to another en route to its destination.

In the United States, the network arranges switching offices in a five-level hierarchy, each level serving a larger geographical area than the level below it. At the bottom are the local offices, the only ones to which telephones are permanently connected. By the mid-1980s there were 19,000 local offices, each directly wired to as few as 100 or as many as 50,000 telephones, and above them 933 toll offices, 168 primary offices, 52 sectional offices and 10 regional offices. Electronic pathways called trunks connect these offices up, down and across the hierarchy.

A call enters the network at the local office. If the number called is nearby, the local office either makes the connection itself or switches the call to the appropriate neighboring local office. If the number indicates a long-distance call, the local office switches the call to a toll office, which searches for the lowest-level unoccupied path to the call's destination. Typically, if that path is busy or if there is no direct connection to another toll office serving the destination phone, it switches the call up one level to a primary office. The call will thus move up through the hierarchy as far as necessary until a path is completed to the destination.

Hierarchical switching has functioned well, but with growing demand, a newer "dynamic" system offers greater flexibility. For example, during morning hours when telephone traffic is heavy in the East but light in the West, dynamic switching might select a roundabout route that bypasses congestion for the Omaha-Tallahassee call illustrated at right. Instead of going through Chicago, the call might be sent to Denver for transmission to Jacksonville and beyond.

Temporary connections in many switching offices *(inset)* may be used to take a hierarchically routed phone call from Omaha to Tallahassee; one possible path is indicated at right. From the caller's home the call travels to a local office, which recognizes it as long distance and sends it on, in this case to the Omaha sectional office. The most direct routes are busy *(yellow lines)*, so Omaha switches the call up to Chicago. Direct lines from Chicago are also busy, so the call goes to Atlanta before making its way to Tallahassee.

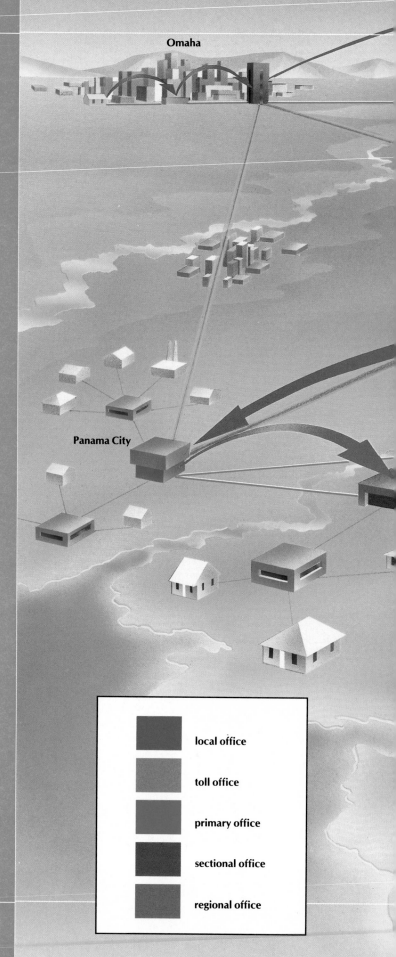

Omaha

Panama City

local office

toll office

primary office

sectional office

regional office

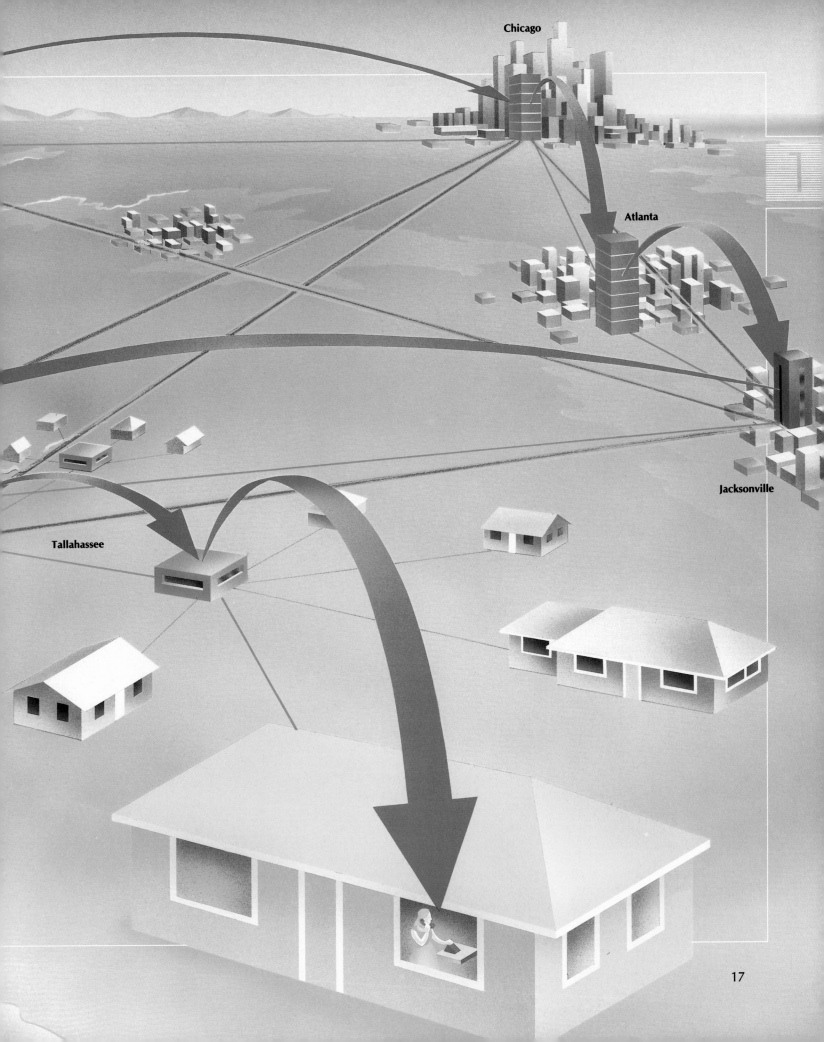

Chicago

Atlanta

Jacksonville

Tallahassee

17

limited to handling data at scarcely one fourth that rate. But the advent of lightning-fast electronic digital computers during and after World War II signaled that modems would have to work at a faster clip.

A major push for greater speed came during the 1950s with the construction of the SAGE air-defense system, the first of the large-scale, computer-centered communications networks. SAGE—for Semi-Automatic Ground Environment—linked hundreds of radar stations in the U.S. and Canada to 27 regional command and control centers. The centers were built around computers modeled after M.I.T.'s Whirlwind, the world's first computer capable of responding in real time—that is, without noticeable delay to the user.

SAGE eventually included approximately 1.5 million miles of communications line. To feed information from the radar stations to the command centers for computer analysis, this huge network needed both new techniques for coding the data in digital form and modems that could transmit it rapidly over telephone lines. In the event that enemy aircraft were detected by the radar network, these modems had to effect the alert virtually instantaneously.

The first high-speed modems were developed by scientists at M.I.T.'s Lincoln Laboratory, which supervised SAGE development for the U.S. Air Force. "At first the telephone company was dubious about what we were doing," recalled Robert R. Everett, a key member of the staff at Lincoln. "When the first telephone line for radar data came into the Whirlwind building to be wired into one of the modems, the telephone installer insisted on wiring it into a handset. We told him we didn't want the handset, but he said it was regulations and that was that. When he left, we connected it to the modem."

SHIFTING INTO HIGH GEAR

Soon, however, engineers and scientists from Bell Labs plunged into research aimed at even faster data transmission. They succeeded in this effort by employing the entire frequency bandwidth of the telephone voice channel instead of dividing it into narrow slices as did the old teletype modems. It is an axiom of telecommunications that the wider the bandwidth of a communications channel, the greater the channel's speed. By the mid-1950s, Bell modems designed specially for SAGE could transmit digital radar data at speeds of up to 1,600 bits per second.

The rigors of meeting SAGE requirements helped prepare Bell researchers for the rising demand for modems and other computer communications technology. Bell's Dataphone system, introduced to the public on a limited basis in 1958, provided the first commercial modems expressly designed for transmitting computer data over ordinary telephone lines. Initially, Dataphone modems could transmit at only about two thirds the rate achieved on the SAGE network. This limitation was imposed largely by the tendency of digital signals to become distorted during transmission. Distortion results in part from different frequencies of a signal traveling over a wire at slightly different speeds, causing a phenomenon that communications engineers call echoes. Over the years, the telephone company had succeeded in reducing the effect of these echoes to the extent that they no longer hindered voice conversations, but the residuum, which made it difficult for a modem to distinguish between ones and zeros in the data stream, was more than enough to ruin computer data. The faster the pace of the data, the shorter the duration of each bit and the more likely a zero will be mistaken for a one or vice versa.

In the SAGE system, engineers were better able to deal with distortion — and thus maintain high-speed transmission — because certain telephone lines were reserved for use exclusively by the system. On dedicated lines such as those, the physical path that the data followed never changed; engineers could analyze distortion in the line and correct it by installing devices called equalizers. The ordinary, switched telephone lines for which the Dataphone modems were intended posed a different problem. On these lines, the physical link between a sender and a receiver had to be established each time a call was made; depending on which circuits were free, the route could be different every time *(pages 16-17)*. Though it was theoretically possible to equalize such a path once it had been established, doing so proved impractical at first. Thus the only way to keep errors within tolerable limits (about one bit in a million) in the Dataphone system was to transmit fewer, longer pulses per second.

A NOVICE'S CHALLENGE

Bell Labs worked steadily on the problem, and in 1964 the lab handed the puzzle to Robert W. Lucky, a 28-year-old electrical engineer. Lucky had been with Bell only three years, and this was the first design problem he had been given to solve, his first opportunity to "create something, invent something." Many years later, Lucky recalled going to a meeting with some of the development people. "They drew a block diagram of this high-speed modem we were supposed to build. There was this empty box labeled 'automatic equalizer.' In the empty box they wrote 'R. W. Lucky.' "

Inspiration for the solution came to Lucky about a month later as he was driving home from work. "I was sitting at this red light," he said, "and it just came to me, the whole thing. And I went home and couldn't sleep. I raced into work with the first light of the sun, and I put it on the computer and naturally it worked perfectly. Sometimes I stop at that light now and wait for an inspiration to hit me. But the light never worked for me again."

Lucky's breakthrough approach to automatic equalization required that the circuits he designed undergo what he called a "training period" of perhaps a second or two after a telephone connection was established. During that time, the originator of the transmission sent out sample pulses at a slow rate. This step was essential, said Lucky, because "in a normal data transmission, you couldn't tell what was an echo and what wasn't; it's all jumbled together." Lucky's equalizer examined the echoes from the widely separated pulses, then generated artificial echoes to counteract the ones responsible for the distortion. Lucky later improved the device so that it could compensate for echoes without a training period and adapt continuously to a telephone circuit's changing electrical characteristics.

Lucky's adaptive equalizer, together with improved techniques for modulating digital signals, opened the way for faster modems. By the early 1970s, Bell Telephone modems were able to transmit data over ordinary switched telephone lines at rates of up to 4,800 bits per second. As it turned out, the adaptive equalizer improved data-transmission speeds over dedicated lines as well. Though such lines feature permanent connections, various electronic factors cause noticeable fluctuations in distortion. Lucky's invention automatically compensated for such variations; earlier techniques could not. Consequently, it became possible to send as many as 9,600 bits per second over dedicated lines, six times the initial speed achieved for SAGE.

MODEMS FOR EVERYONE

By the time these data-transmission speeds were realized, modems had become easily portable, having shrunk from their original bulkiness — approximately the size of a small refrigerator — to the compact dimensions of a cigar box. Some models were built onto circuit boards that slipped inside desktop computers. And the marvels of computer miniaturization made it likely that the modem would find its way onto a single computer chip.

The trend toward portable modems began in the 1960s. At that time, a modem was built into the computer terminal and then permanently connected to the telephone lines. When users wanted to move the machine to a new location in the office, they had to call in the phone company to make expensive new connections.

Confronted with this inconvenience in his own office, John Van Geen did something about it. In 1966, Van Geen was a 37-year-old engineer at California's Stanford Research Institute (now SRI International). He and other researchers were connected through Bell's TWX teletype network to the pioneering computer time-sharing service a continent away at Dartmouth College. Every time Van Geen or his colleagues wanted to hook up with the computer to make mathematical computations, they had to walk to the terminal's permanent installation at the end of a hallway. The machine was too expensive for everybody to have one.

One way around the problem was to build a modem that could use a telephone as the link to the network. With such a device, the permanent wiring between the terminal and the TWX network would no longer be necessary; a terminal could be rolled to any office, where it could be connected to an ordinary phone line. When Van Geen began his work on this idea, there were a number of such modems on the market. Typically, the connection to the terminal was made by wires fastened to the same attachment points that the built-in modem had used; the connection to the telephone was made by a device known as an acoustic coupler, which had sound-deadening receptacles for the mouthpiece and earpiece of a standard telephone handset. The modem converted digital signals from the terminal into analog signals for the telephone network and sent them out through the mouthpiece to Dartmouth. Results from the computer, arriving through the earpiece, were demodulated and then — in an era when television-like computer screens were rare — printed like a telegram.

Van Geen, however, found the existing modems lacking; they worked well for links to nearby computers but functioned unpredictably over long-distance telephone lines, such as those connecting Van Geen and his colleagues to the computer in New Hampshire. The modems could not distinguish reliably between the weak data signal that arrived in California after a 3,000-mile journey and the noise that accompanied the information. Consequently, data received from the computer contained an unacceptable number of errors.

In his own device, Van Geen retained in principle the acoustic coupler and transmitter from current modems and then went on to solve the reception problem by incorporating a different type of receiver in his modem, one that tolerated wide variations in signal strength and noise. It was so successful that he was able to receive virtually error-free data over distances as great as 6,000 miles.

Even so, some errors could be introduced into the modem by loud sounds nearby, which were able to penetrate the sound-deadening material of the acoustic coupler. Such errors might have been eliminated had Van Geen wired his modem directly to the telephone system. But in 1966, such a connection would have been illegal. At that time, telephone-company rules called tariffs, in addition to establishing rates, prohibited connecting to the telephone network any devices not furnished by the phone company. The argument against so-called foreign equipment was that it might damage the network; the penalty for ignoring this rule could be termination of telephone service.

Nonetheless, Van Geen and his colleagues worked closely with the telephone company to ensure that his modem's transmitter would exactly mimic the signals sent out by Bell's modem, thus defusing the potential charge that Van Geen's device would generate signals incompatible with the network. Moreover, because the new modem caused no harm — and because the phone company saw the possibility of increased revenues from the growth of data transmission — no action was taken to halt its use.

In 1968, two years after Van Geen's acoustic-coupled modem appeared, the Federal Communications Commission (FCC) issued a ruling that ended the tariffs' strangle hold on the use of foreign equipment. In this far-reaching decision, the manufacturers of a device called the Carterphone, which linked two-way radios and telephones, prevailed over the telephone company. As a result, AT&T could no longer ban equipment from other suppliers, although it retained the right to insert protective circuitry between such products and the AT&T network. By 1977, even that restriction was dropped as the FCC inaugurated a program of certification for telephone equipment. Any device that conformed to certain published standards could now be plugged directly into the network.

The Carterphone decision spawned an entire industry devoted to the manufacture of telephone-related equipment, from ordinary phones to sophisticated office communications systems. As for modems, competition soon made them smaller, faster and cheaper. In the early 1980s, as personal computers proliferated, sales of modems soared. Ultimately, the modem — etched onto a single, integrated-circuit chip — may become a standard feature of computers.

A BOX BRIMMING WITH POTENTIAL

It is little wonder that modems have become so popular. A modem is a computer's umbilical cord to the world. For example, about a quarter of a million workers in the United States are now computing — rather than commuting — to the office. Few computer accessories offer so many possibilities for so little money. Whether the modem in question is connected to a multimillion-dollar business computer or to a modest computer in the home, it opens the door to a vast smorgasbord of information, services and opportunities. To have a computer and a modem is to be an armchair adventurer.

In the United States, the adventure is fostered by scores of private enterprises. Two of the largest, CompuServe and The Source, offer many of the services and conveniences found in any community. For a one-time subscription fee — plus

Hexagons for a Mobile Phone Network

A simplified cellular telephone system is laid out in a honeycomb of hexagonal cells, each with FM radio transmitters linking the land-based "wire line" telephone network to mobile units within the cell. Ideally, each cell has at its center one station with an antenna (insets) atop a 100- to 300-foot tower. The transmission covers an approximately circular area. (The hexagonal shape of the cell closely matches a circle while eliminating the gaps and overlaps that circular cells would introduce.) The cell station relays signals to and from the mobile unit, and also helps control its operation.

"When Hollywood Calls, It Will Likely Be from the Driver's Seat of a Cruising Car," headlined The Wall Street Journal, reporting on the entertainment industry's passion for cellular phones, an improved automobile-telephone system that enables a phone in a car to communicate with almost any other phone in the world. Within two years after cellular phones first became available in Southern California, some 55,000 had been installed (at $1,000 or more apiece). As costs decline, the telephone may become as common an automobile accessory as the stereo tape deck.

Automobile telephones had long been available to the public, but in very limited numbers. They must be connected by radio channels — one per conversation — to a "land station," and until 1980 just 44 channels were available in the U.S. Such a service in Chicago was able to handle only about 2,000 subscribers, all sharing lines; the waiting list for a car phone in some areas stretched to 15 years. But with the advent of the cellular system, which allows each channel to be reused many times, and with an increase in the number of available channels to 666, car-phone subscriptions have become virtually unlimited.

The trick to multiple use involves, first, the employment of low-power transmitters and receivers instead of the high-power ones previously used. Second, transmission is restrict-ed to a small area, or cell *(below)*, instead of the 75-mile spacing that had been common. Finally, multiple use depends on computer systems that automatically select the channel for a call, then switch channels in midconversation if the car phone moves out of one channel's range and into another's. Under these conditions, adjacent cells must use different channels, but nonadjacent cells, even when separated only by a short distance, can use the same channels without interference. Because this cellular system can be applied not just to car phones but to any portable telephone, it could eventually bring about personal communications devices as convenient and wearable as a wristwatch.

Subdividing to Serve a Host of Callers

Generally, each cell in the telephone system is assigned a group of 50 to 70 radio channels — enough for that many simultaneous conversations within the cell. Adjacent cells must use different groups of channels, indicated here by different colors, to avoid interference. But nonadjacent cells can use the same groups *(matching colors)*, thus allowing a limited number of channels to be used again and again to serve many subscribers. In busy areas, cells can be subdivided into smaller ones, each with 50 to 70 channels and lower-power cell stations.

Shifting the Station to Suit the Cell

Although in the ideal setup the cell-station antenna is centrally located, it may have to be placed elsewhere to reduce interference where cells are small and close together. In this example, one antenna at a corner covers parts of three cells. It is directional — designed so that it sends a different group of channels *(colors)* into each of the three cells shown at left. The remaining areas of these cells must be covered by other directional antennas *(not shown)*.

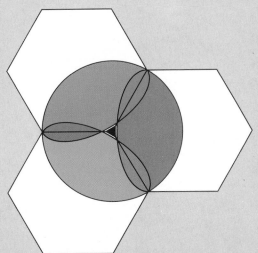

Making Connections to a Cruising Car

THE HAND-OFF: KEEPING IN TOUCH CROSS-COUNTRY

The unique feature of cellular systems is automatic switching of a call between channels and cell stations as a car travels from cell to cell. Here, an office *(yellow building)* communicates with a car via exchange *(blue)*, MSC *(black)* and cell station *(below)*. As the car moves to the edge of the first cell, its signal to that station fades. The MSC, which monitors signals picked up by all cell stations, finds that the car signal comes in stronger in an adjacent cell *(below, right)* and orders the car phone to switch to a channel in the new cell. This hand-off usually takes a fifth of a second; the break in the conversation is undetectable.

One car is traveling somewhere in the hundreds of square miles covered by the Los Angeles cellular telephone system. Another is somewhere in the Washington-Baltimore system. No one but the drivers knows exactly where either car is, yet they can be connected by telephone almost as quickly and easily as if they were seated at their office desks.

This electronic legerdemain is performed partly by the mobile telephone itself, partly by the cell stations and partly by the Mobile Switching Center (MSC), which includes a computer system linking the regular telephone central exchange with the cell stations. The MSC and the cell stations work together to pick up transmissions from car phones making calls and to page phones being called, tuning them to channels available from the nearest cell stations, retuning them to

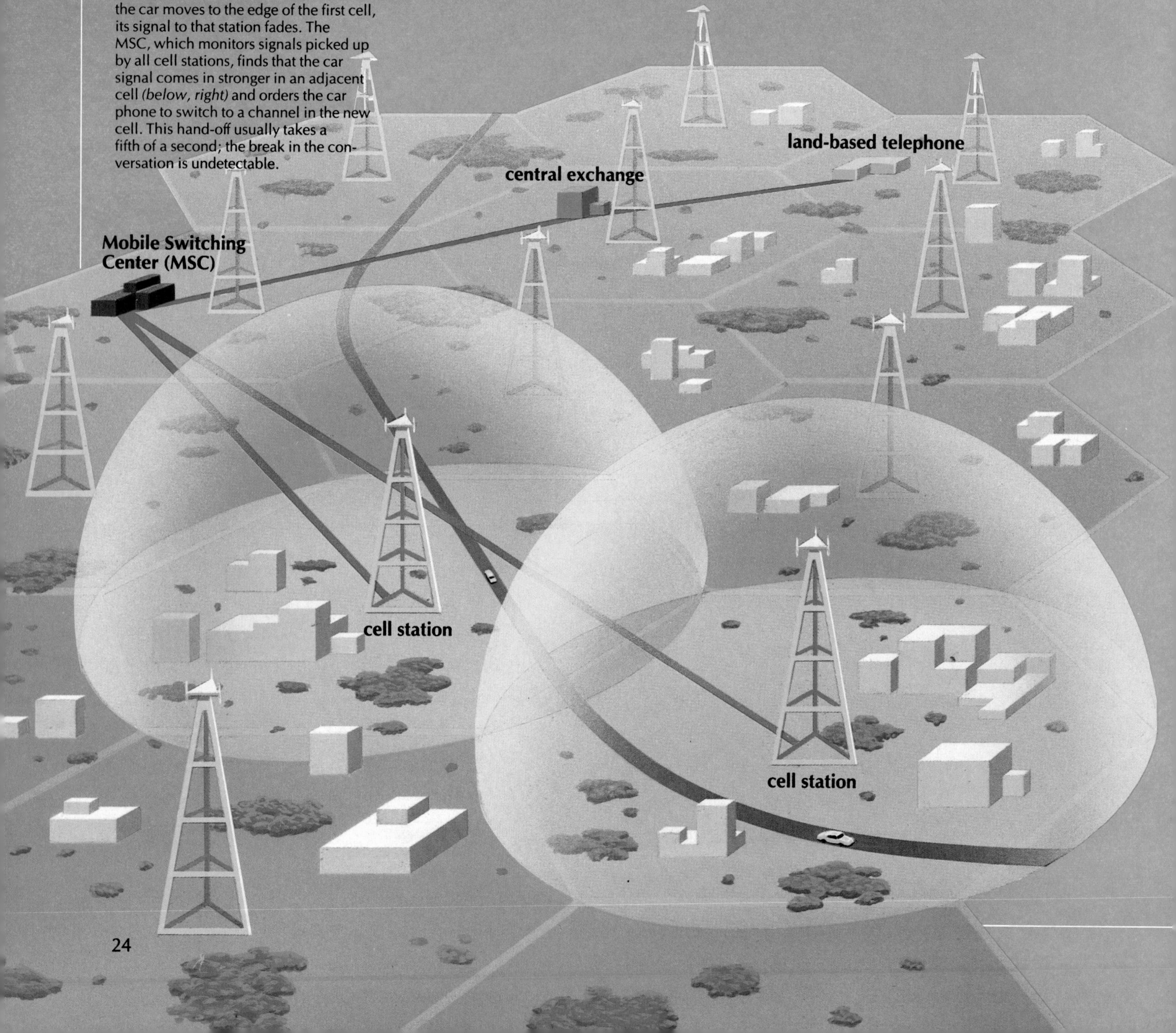

land-based telephone

central exchange

Mobile Switching Center (MSC)

cell station

cell station

other stations' channels when they move out of range of the first and connecting them to the regular land-based telephone network as required. The MSC and the cell stations also check the car phones' serial numbers and keep track of the bills.

How the system works can be seen by tracing a call from an office building to a car in the local area *(below, left)*; long-distance calls and calls between cars *(below, right)* or from car to land telephone are handled similarly. In the first example, the office-bound caller simply dials the desired mobile-telephone number. The local central exchange passes that number on to the MSC, which sends it to all cell stations in the area. The cell stations transmit the number over special channels set aside for control signals.

Meanwhile, the car telephone — switched on but not in use — scans the control channels and locks on to the one that comes in strongest, that is, the one in the cell the car happens to be traveling through. When the car phone, monitoring that control channel, picks up its number, it signals an acknowledgment back over the same channel to tell the computer system which cell the car is in. The system then tunes the car phone to a speaking channel for the call — one of the 50 to 70 channels assigned to the car's cell but not presently being used. Now the connection is completed and the phone rings.

As the car moves from one cell to another, signals to and from the first cell station fade while those to and from the next cell station strengthen. The computer system senses the change and automatically hands off the call to an available channel in the cell the car is entering.

TELEPHONING ON THE ROAD, TRAVELER TO TRAVELER

When a subscriber on the road dials another car phone, the number is relayed to the MSC via the caller's cell station, and a channel is assigned to the calling phone. The MSC now pages all cells to locate the unit being called. When the unit responds, the system assigns the called unit a channel and links the two so that conversation may begin. The parties may talk indefinitely, while the MSC repeatedly hands them off to new channels whenever they cross cell boundaries.

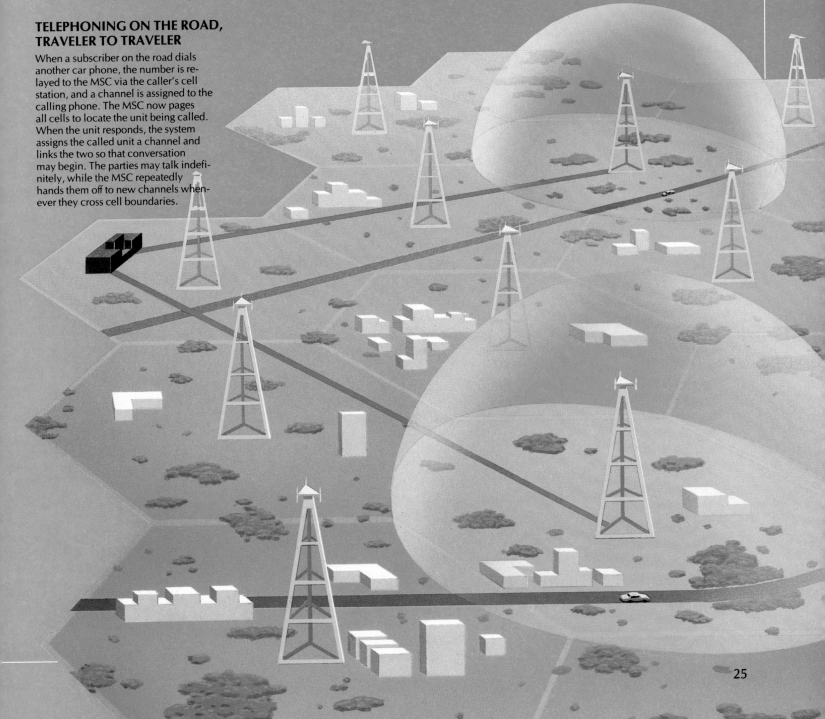

charges assessed according to the length of time the user is connected to the system — customers of such services can shop and make travel reservations. Elsewhere on the system, they can swap messages with other subscribers by means of a computerized postal system.

A few keystrokes away, dozens of data bases brim with information of all kinds. Entire encyclopedias and up-to-the-minute stock-market quotations, news and weather are only the start of it. Dialog Information Services is the largest of the on-line data bases. It contains more than 100 million records, including references to articles in 10,000 journals and to every one of the millions of books in the Library of Congress. Most data bases specialize. Legi-Slate, for example, offers an instant check on the current status of any bill in the U.S. Congress and on the voting record of any member of the House or Senate since 1979. NewsNet contains the complete text of more than 200 newsletters on subjects ranging from tobacco exports to organized religion.

TOO MUCH INFORMATION EQUALS NONE

Using one of these data bases can be perplexing. Because of the amount of information they contain, they tend to be labyrinthine. Costs can mount as the quest progresses, and if a search is too broad, the result can be a swirling inundation of data so voluminous as to be useless. One magazine writer's experience illustrates the possibilities. He was searching Nexis, a data base that contains the text of newspaper and magazine articles, to learn what then U.S. Treasury Secretary Donald Regan had been saying to the press about his work. More to prove to himself the vastness of this 3.8-billion-word data base than to make a serious attempt at information retrieval, he first asked for all the news stories on record in which "Regan" and "Treasury" appeared within 30 words of each other. This kind of request is called a proximity search, and the result was a deluge of 17,251 citations. Narrowing his request to include only those articles in which the words "deficit" and "interest" appeared in close proximity to the words of his first attempt, he was rewarded with a mere 1,239 stories. By further specifying that he was interested in stories written within the preceding 10 weeks or so, he was rewarded with 14 recent references, a much more manageable number.

Other telecomputing tasks are less demanding than searching a data base. One of the simplest and most widely used services is electronic mail, or E-mail, which is offered by a half dozen or more nationwide networks and, on a local basis, by hundreds of corporations, colleges and other institutions. A subscriber prepares the message on a computer in the office and then transmits it to the mail service's host computer. There, the message, which might be as short as a thank-you note or as long as a manuscript for a novel, is stored in the electronic mailbox — actually space on a data-storage disk — of the addressee, who collects the mail by having it forwarded to his own terminal.

For all its speed and convenience, E-mail has its drawbacks. Not every office worker has a computer, and not all electronic-mail enthusiasts subscribe to the same service — a reminder of the chaotic early days of the telephone when, in order to be able to reach everyone in town, people often had to become customers of more than one telephone company. Moreover, some messages simply do not lend themselves to electronic mail. "If you are trying to negotiate something, or express strong emotions, then the telephone is very effective," says one high-technology consultant. "There is an interactive give-and-take, with subtle voice signals, that can't be mimicked adequately by electronic mail."

Yet, many who communicate by computer do find ways to express emotion. Some simulate shouting by typing all capital letters. For others, E-mail provides emotional distance that permits them to overcome initial shyness. Two Princeton students met through the campus electronic-mail service and eventually married. "We had never really talked to each other," explained the bride. "We started writing letters, and then flirting in the letters. I don't think we could have done that in person. The computer bridged the gap."

Closely related to E-mail — and sometimes overlapping it — is the electronic bulletin board. The big supermarkets of information and services, such as CompuServe and The Source, sponsor numerous bulletin boards, but the concept best shows off its fascinating diversity at the grassroots level. Thousands of home-grown bulletin boards flourish as clearinghouses for public notices and messages, and as arenas for swapping lively ideas or computer software that has been placed in the public domain by generous programmers. A bulletin board in Berkeley, California, is unusual in that it serves people who lack a computer. Terminals for the network are installed in stores and restaurants, where about 1,200 people a month can take advantage of the service for purposes ranging from posting electronic notices about cars for sale and apartments for rent to exercising their right to sound off on any topic they choose. The network is provided free of charge by the Community Memory Project, which was established in the early 1970s — before the arrival of the personal computer — to introduce ordinary people to the power of computers. One of its founders was Lee Felsenstein, a legendary figure in those days; among other accomplishments, he designed the Osborne portable computer, one of the earliest personal computers intended to be carried from place to place. Community Memory's bulletin board is financed largely by royalties from software written by the project's founders, including the program that runs the network itself.

HIGH-TECH POPULIST

An outspoken advocate of computer communications in general is David Hughes. A town planner and retired army colonel in Colorado Springs, Colorado, Hughes has called himself "a citizen of the information age." He runs a bulletin board called Old Colorado's Electronic Cottage and has consulted professionally with city officials across the country by computer. He has published on The Source his own electronic magazine, described by a journalist as "one part modern-day Will Rogers, one part high-tech Rod McKuen and two parts pearls of philosophy about the age of personal computing." He has taught a course in writing, electronically mailing lectures and assignments to students as far away as Australia, who paid $100 tuition and earned college credit for their efforts. Hughes has lobbied strenuously against threats to what he has called his "electronic freedom of speech." When city planners in Colorado Springs proposed a zoning change that would have restricted the use of computers for working at home by allowing only one residence-based occupation per household, he used his bulletin board to mobilize opposition to the measure. Nearly 200 people showed up at the next city-council meeting to voice their protests on an issue that had not even made the news. The proposed change was modified to suit them. "That's pure populism at work," Hughes said afterward. "Tom Paine would have first published 'Common Sense' on a computer bulletin board."

COMMUNICATING BY THE GROUP

Electronic bulletin boards may be a versatile tool for community action, but they suffer from a serious limitation; at best, they are a disappointing medium for dialogue. Much more satisfactory is a computerized version of a conference call known as a teleconference. In the U.S., a dozen or so different commercial services arrange computer get-togethers for groups that wish to exchange information. One type of teleconferencing resembles citizens-band radio. Participants in this so-called CB Simulator tune into the same "channel," where a remark typed at one terminal appears on the computer screens of all the participants. People from all over the country—each with a personal "handle," or special name—gather to chat about matters large and small or about mutual interests such as a particular computer language or perhaps the problems of child rearing.

Far more common is a style of teleconference that does not require the simultaneous presence of all participants. In this flexible arrangement, members of the conference join in at their convenience, review the progress of the electronic meeting since the last time they were present, respond to specific messages, update information and ask questions of any participants, who reply when they next check on the progress of the conference. Corporations find this type of teleconferencing useful. It brings people together without restrictions on time or location and keeps a faultless record of the proceedings.

With the ability to communicate in this fashion, determined conferees can get a job done quickly. In 1980, engine trouble forced down a helicopter in a remote region of Nepal. No one was injured, but without a new engine the crew and passengers, a group of physicians on a United Nations project, would be stranded for weeks. The only replacement engine available was 4,200 miles away in France. Arrangements for shipping it to Nepal required elaborate consultations among the bureaucracies of four far-flung organizations in different time zones: the U.N. in New York; the World Health Organization in New Delhi; a Michigan-based nonprofit foundation that was funding the project; and the government of Nepal. The parties consulted over an international computer-conferencing system. In less than a day on-line, all the wrinkles were ironed out and agreement was reached on such potentially troublesome questions as who would pay for the engine and how it would be transported to one of the earth's most inaccessible corners. A few days later, the new engine was installed and the physicians flew out of Nepal, able to continue their work thanks to this extraordinary electronic forum.

Analog or Digital: The Dual Face of Communications

Just by punching a few buttons on a telephone or a computer keyboard, someone in Des Moines can in seconds be talking via satellite to Hong Kong or scrolling through quotations on the London stock exchange. This technological wizardry is made possible by communications networks so complex that no one person, not even among the engineers most familiar with their workings, can trace a particular message through every switch, amplifier, filter, cable, wave guide, laser beam, radio wave and satellite that links the message's sender to its recipient.

For all this impenetrable complexity, the telecommunications network operates on fairly simple principles. It uses signals of electromagnetic energy — electric currents, radio waves and light beams — to carry messages. Both the information in the messages and the signals used for transmitting them can be lumped into two broad categories: analog and digital.

In essence, an analog signal is continuous and a digital one is discontinuous. Both analog and digital signals can carry messages made up of either analog or digital data. However, before analog information can be sent by digital means, it must be broken into discrete chunks. Similarly, to send digital data by analog means, the individual chunks of digital data must be loaded onto a continuous carrier signal.

For most of its history, the telephone system — the dominant element in global telecommunications — has been analog in nature. The majority of telephone facilities still carry the human voice on an analog signal — an electronic facsimile, in effect, of the continuously varying sound waves of speech. Today's telephone system, however, is increasingly used to carry computer-generated digital information as well — and tomorrow's system will be expressly built for this expanding traffic, so that the human voice will have to be translated from analog to digital form before gaining entry.

The conversion of the telephone system will take until early in the 21st century. Yet even as a transitional patchwork of analog and digital components, the network is so versatile and reliable that it ranks as a wonder of the modern world.

Variations on an Electronic Theme

The difference between the two basic forms of electronic communication, analog and digital, is a little like the difference between water streaming from a hose and bullets firing from a machine gun. An analog signal is a continuous electromagnetic wave, whose pattern varies to represent the message being transmitted. A digital signal, by contrast, is a series of discrete electronic bursts; again, the pattern created by the bursts indicates the message.

Most telephones work by copying the variations of sound waves generated at the transmitting end onto analog elec-

ELECTRONIC ANALOGS FOR SOUND

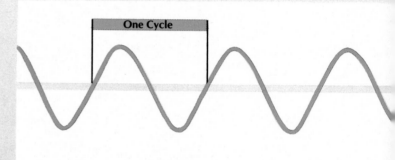

One Cycle

Key characteristics of an analog signal include strength, or amplitude (vertical distance between a wave trough and crest) and frequency (the number of times per second the wave cycle repeats). The wave shown above is a sine wave, representative of a pure tone.

ELECTRONIC PULSES FOR BINARY DIGITS

OFF	ON	OFF	OFF	OFF	OFF	OFF	ON
0	1	0	0	0	0	0	1

BIT

BYTE

Computer messages are composed of bytes, or groups of binary digits (here, eight), conveyed in this simple example as the presence or absence of voltage in an electronic signal. For the byte above, the voltage goes successively off, on, off, off, off, off, off, on.

tromagnetic waves, which are converted back to sound waves when they arrive at the receiving end. The specific qualities of a sound — its loudness and its pitch, for example — depend on the waves' amplitude, or strength, and on their frequency, or how closely together waves are spaced (measured in cycles per second, called hertz).

A computer, on the other hand, "talks" to other computers in streams of binary digits, or bits — 1s and 0s. Bits may be transmitted simply as a digital signal: an electromagnetic pulse of a given voltage for a 1, a pulse of a significantly different — usually weaker — voltage for a 0.

Digital signals have several important advantages over analog ones. They can be transmitted over cheaper equipment. They are also less prone to error. In an analog signal, deviations in amplitude or frequency are apt to occur over long distances, changing the signal pattern — and thus distorting the message. But even a substantial deviation in a digital pulse would not prevent it from being recognized as representing either a 1 or a 0; the pattern of the signal — and the message — is preserved.

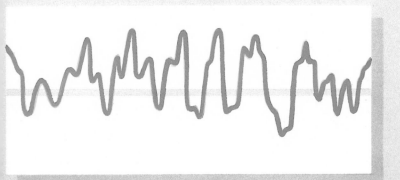

In this graph of a typical analog signal, the many variations in amplitude and frequency convey the gradations of loudness and pitch in speech or music. Similar signals are used to transmit television pictures, but at much higher frequencies.

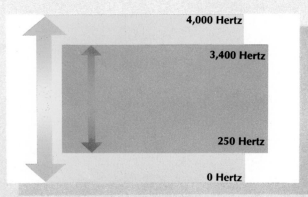

The human voice creates waves of many frequencies, but natural-sounding speech can be limited to a frequency range, or band, of 250 to 3,400 cycles per second. Telephone equipment allows the voice a bandwidth of 4,000 hertz, which includes a guard band at top and bottom to prevent interference. TV signals need a bandwidth of four million hertz (4 MHZ).

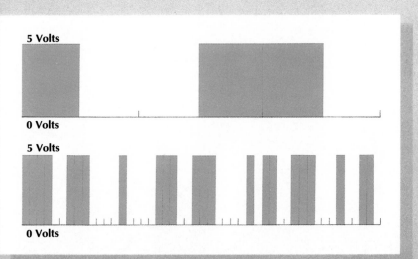

Two digital signals, each made up of 0s (zero volts, white spaces) and 1s (five-volt pulses, orange bars), are depicted as transmitted at different rates over a 1/50-second interval. The top signal carries 300 bits per second (bps), the bottom one 2,400 bps.

31

Techniques for Sharing a Circuit

If every message had to move single file through every link in the global telecommunications network — like bicyclists on a narrow path — communications would be hopelessly slow. But if at some point the bicyclists can be loaded onto buses and sent down a multilane highway, traffic is enormously speeded. That, in effect, is what happens when many signals from telephones or computers reach a local central office on their way across a big city or across the planet. This "multiplexing" allows multiple streams of electronic messages to be transmitted over the same connection in the time otherwise required for one message.

Multiplexing is effected in two major ways: frequency-

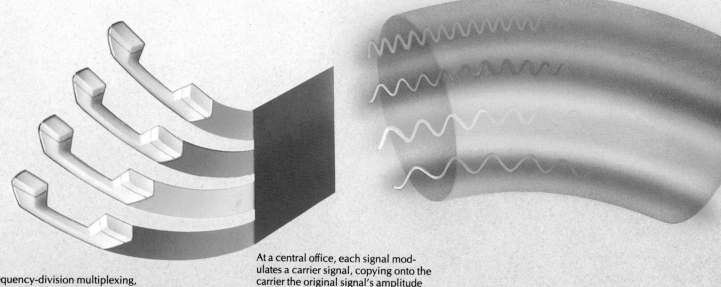

In frequency-division multiplexing, each signal — from a telephone, for example — travels on its own line to the central office, where signals are combined for distant transmission.

At a central office, each signal modulates a carrier signal, copying onto the carrier the original signal's amplitude variations. For simplicity, the stacked carriers above are shown unmodulated.

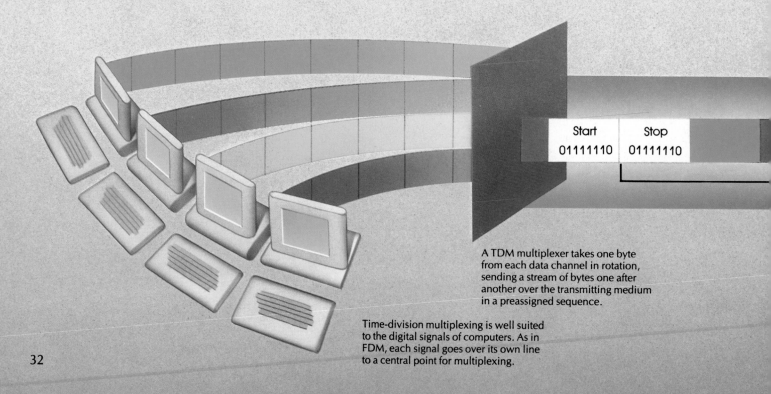

Start	Stop
01111110	01111110

A TDM multiplexer takes one byte from each data channel in rotation, sending a stream of bytes one after another over the transmitting medium in a preassigned sequence.

Time-division multiplexing is well suited to the digital signals of computers. As in FDM, each signal goes over its own line to a central point for multiplexing.

division multiplexing (FDM) and time-division multiplexing (TDM). The older of the two, FDM, is used with analog transmission. The analog signal is impressed on another analog signal of different frequency — a carrier — altering the carrier's shape so that it bears the pattern of the message. The carrier frequency generally remains constant; only its amplitude varies, at a rate corresponding to that of the message signal. Since each carrier has a different frequency, carriers can be stacked one atop the other and sent together over a cable or microwave radio link capable of carrying a broad range of frequencies; the carriers are then separated at the other end. The greater the medium's bandwidth, the more carriers it can transmit, and the more messages it can handle simultaneously.

Time-division multiplexing operates by a kind of round robin, employing a device that scans individual channels in rotation — taking a byte from each channel and transmitting the bytes in a string, according to a sequence determined at the outset. In the TDM method, each byte is also condensed so that many can be sent during the time ordinarily required for one: Each byte is briefly stored in a buffer, then released as a series of much shorter pulses, leaving a space of unused time between series. Into these spaces, similarly condensed bytes from other channels can be inserted.

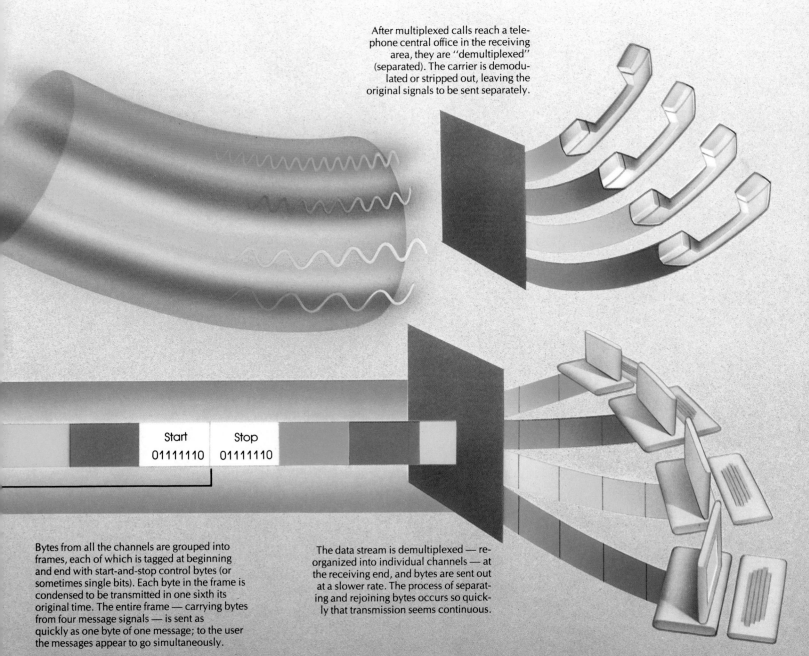

After multiplexed calls reach a telephone central office in the receiving area, they are "demultiplexed" (separated). The carrier is demodulated or stripped out, leaving the original signals to be sent separately.

Start	Stop
01111110	01111110

Bytes from all the channels are grouped into frames, each of which is tagged at beginning and end with start-and-stop control bytes (or sometimes single bits). Each byte in the frame is condensed to be transmitted in one sixth its original time. The entire frame — carrying bytes from four message signals — is sent as quickly as one byte of one message; to the user the messages appear to go simultaneously.

The data stream is demultiplexed — reorganized into individual channels — at the receiving end, and bytes are sent out at a slower rate. The process of separating and rejoining bytes occurs so quickly that transmission seems continuous.

Putting Pulses onto Waves

A computer user who wants to gain access to a distant data bank or chat on the screen with fellow users generally depends on the telephone system, the only electronic connection available almost everywhere. But most of the telephone system is designed for analog signals; the digital pulses from a computer are badly distorted by electrical characteristics of the twisted wires that make up an ordinary phone line, and the digital signals can travel no more than a couple of thousand yards before becoming hopelessly garbled. This dilemma is

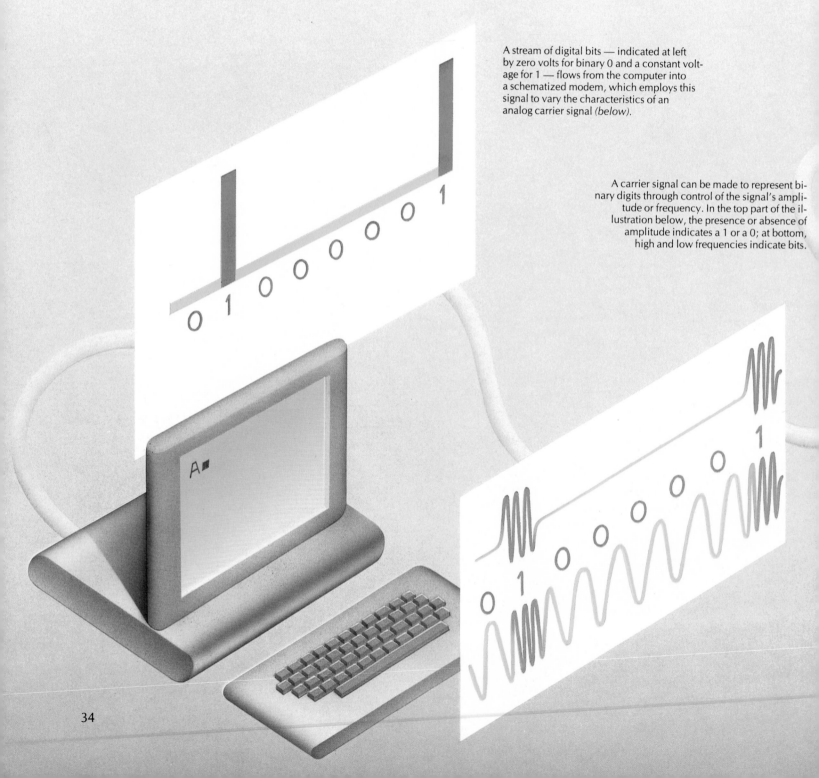

A stream of digital bits — indicated at left by zero volts for binary 0 and a constant voltage for 1 — flows from the computer into a schematized modem, which employs this signal to vary the characteristics of an analog carrier signal *(below)*.

A carrier signal can be made to represent binary digits through control of the signal's amplitude or frequency. In the top part of the illustration below, the presence or absence of amplitude indicates a 1 or a 0; at bottom, high and low frequencies indicate bits.

resolved with a modulator-demodulator, or modem, which puts the pulses of digital data into the form of an analog wave.

A modem uses digital signals to modulate an analog carrier signal, changing one or another of several wave characteristics to correspond to pulses. In one method, amplitude-shift keying, the modem changes the wave so that it produces two different amplitudes—one amplitude for binary 1, another for binary 0. In the more common frequency-shift keying, the modem generates two differ-ent frequencies, one frequency for a 1, another for a 0.

The small, low-speed modem most familiar to personal-computer users works by frequency-shift keying: It converts the computer's digital signals into a series of frequency tones audible as beeps and bips, then transmits them. Modems of this type are reliable but relatively slow, with a top transmission speed of about 1,200 bits per second. Much higher speeds are attainable with modems that take advantage of other characteristics of the analog signal *(page 53)*.

At the receiving end, the analog signal must be demodulated, or changed back into the only form a computer can understand — the two-state, on-off binary code. Below, a frequency-modulated signal passes through a schematized modem and resumes its original form, a series of electrical pulses in which the presence or absence of voltage represents a 1 or a 0.

0 1 0 0 0 0 0 1

A

Converting a Voice to Ones and Zeros

While telephone companies rush to reap the benefits of digital communication, converting their systems from analog to digital, they must still handle their traditional business of transmitting the human voice — which is fundamentally an analog phenomenon. The varying sounds of human speech must first be transformed into discrete pulses to be sent by digital means. The device for making this transformation is called a codec, a name derived from its function of coding an analog signal into digital form at the sending end and then decoding it back to analog form at the receiving end. Codecs have been used

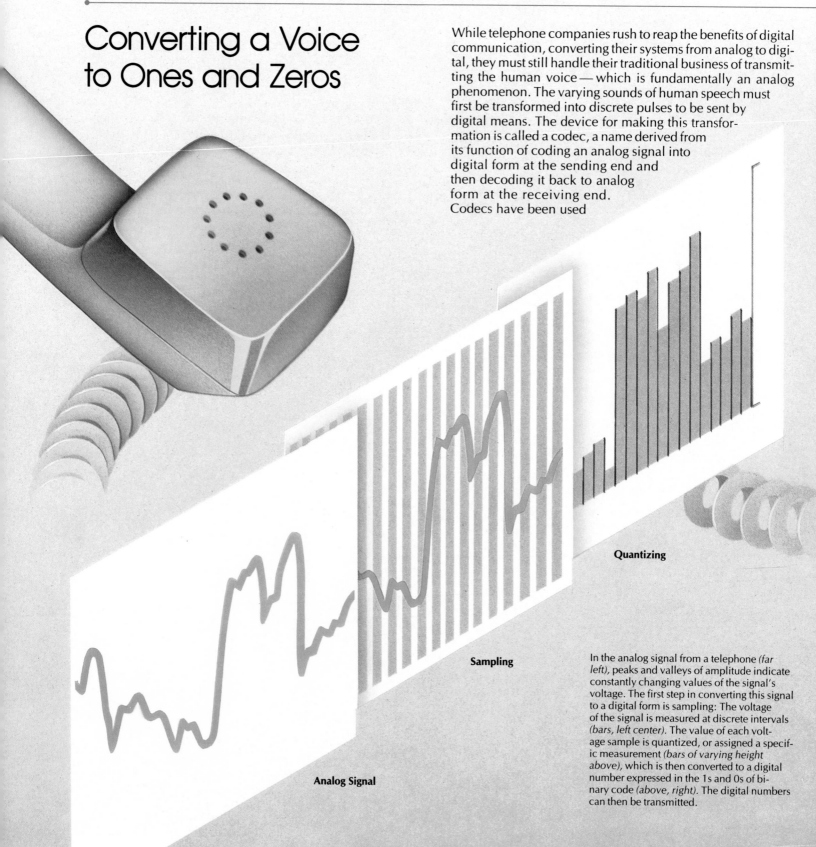

Quantizing

Sampling

Analog Signal

In the analog signal from a telephone *(far left)*, peaks and valleys of amplitude indicate constantly changing values of the signal's voltage. The first step in converting this signal to a digital form is sampling: The voltage of the signal is measured at discrete intervals *(bars, left center)*. The value of each voltage sample is quantized, or assigned a specific measurement *(bars of varying height above)*, which is then converted to a digital number expressed in the 1s and 0s of binary code *(above, right)*. The digital numbers can then be transmitted.

mainly at central offices for routing calls over main trunk lines, but telephones may eventually have codecs built into their handsets so that calls are digitized from the start. This will obviate numerous conversions and reconversions between analog and digital, and the entire communications network will be able to take advantage of the lower costs, higher fidelity and error-resistance of digital transmission.

A codec accomplishes its task in three stages. The first is sampling the amplitude of the analog signal at very short intervals. The next is quantizing, or assigning decimal values to the amplitude samples. The result is known as pulse amplitude modulation (PAM). In the final stage, known as pulse code modulation (PCM), the voltage values are converted, or coded, into binary numbers for digital transmission.

To make sure that speech remains intelligible, a great many samples must be taken. The sampling rate — according to a rule discovered about half a century ago by Harry Nyquist of Bell Laboratories — must be twice that of the highest significant frequency to be transmitted. Thus, for a voice signal, with an upper frequency limit of 4,000 hertz over the phone system, the codec must take 8,000 samples per second. The speech lost between samples, known as the Nyquist interval, is unnoticeable when the signal is decoded at the receiving end.

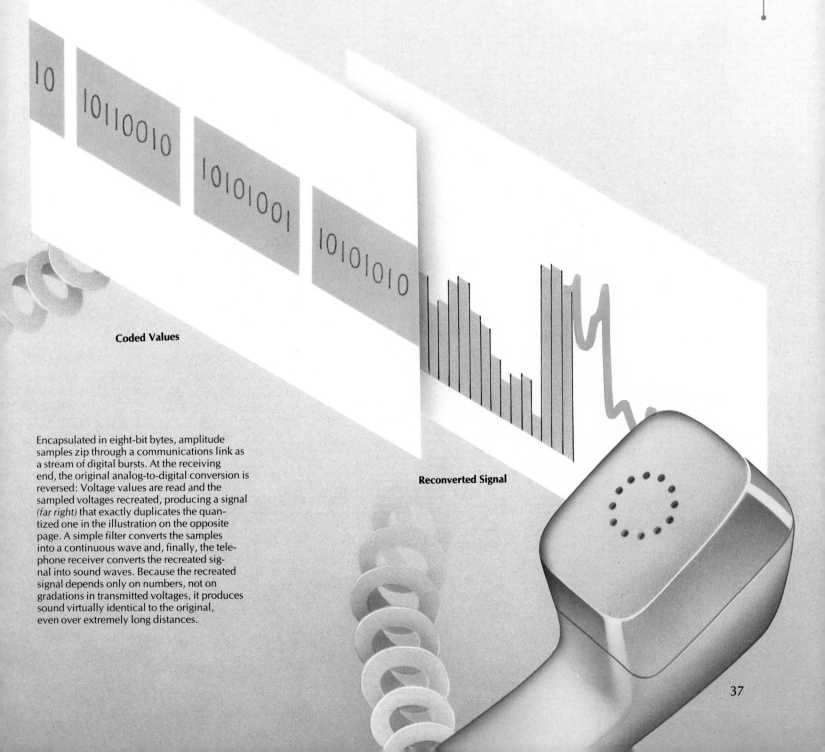

Coded Values

Reconverted Signal

Encapsulated in eight-bit bytes, amplitude samples zip through a communications link as a stream of digital bursts. At the receiving end, the original analog-to-digital conversion is reversed: Voltage values are read and the sampled voltages recreated, producing a signal *(far right)* that exactly duplicates the quantized one in the illustration on the opposite page. A simple filter converts the samples into a continuous wave and, finally, the telephone receiver converts the recreated signal into sound waves. Because the recreated signal depends only on numbers, not on gradations in transmitted voltages, it produces sound virtually identical to the original, even over extremely long distances.

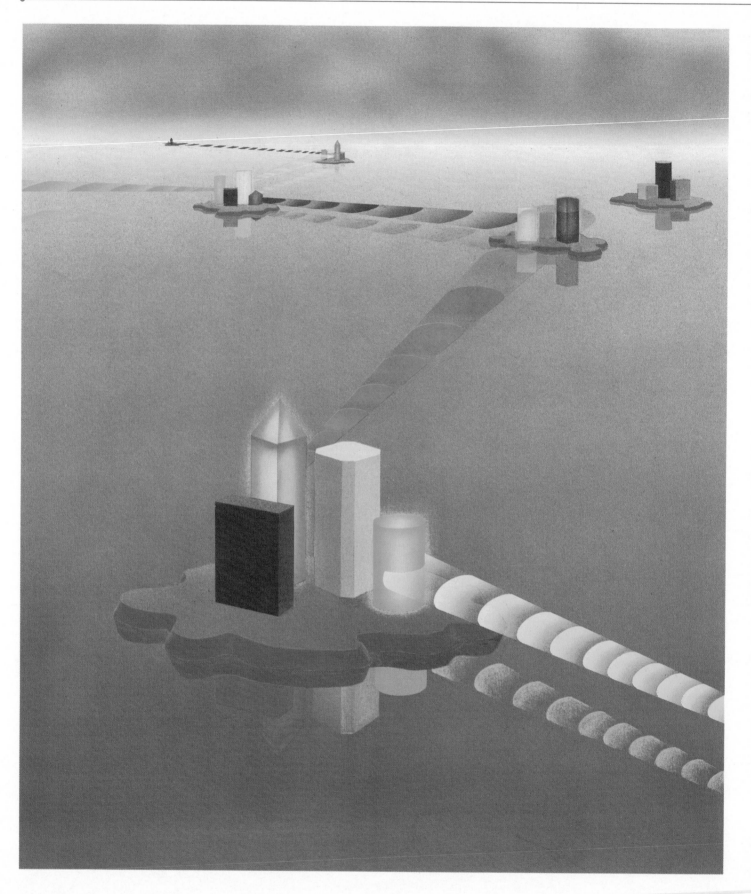

Expanding Horizons with Networks

Late in 1965, an innovative computer service made its debut in suburban Boston. Keydata Corporation, in existence only a couple of years, leased dumb terminals—ones having a display screen and a keyboard, but devoid of computing power—to some 20 businesses throughout the metropolitan area and linked the terminals to a Univac 491 mainframe computer situated in the university town of Cambridge. Through these terminals, Keydata's Univac provided computerized invoicing and inventory control for companies ranging from liquor distributors to a book publisher. The terminals communicated with the Univac by modem, over leased telephone lines. For the first time, a business could gain access to a computer almost as conveniently as making a phone call—and much more economically than by owning one of those prohibitively priced machines or renting it for exclusive use.

The means to this end was a new technology called time sharing. Special software enabled the computer, called the host in this kind of system, to share its computing power among hundreds of terminals located some distance away. In essence, the computer rapidly shifted its attention from terminal to terminal. At each stop, it performed—in a tiny fraction of a second—a small part of the task in progress there, giving the impression to anyone working with the system that he or she was the only person using it. Clients, calling up their own custom-designed programs, could send information to the Univac from the terminal keyboard and watch seconds later as the computer instructed a printer near the terminal to type an invoice or an inventory report.

Keydata did not invent computer time sharing. During the early 1960s, a number of companies and universities investigated time sharing independently, and several such operations already were under way by 1965. They had been established largely for the science and engineering communities or by huge companies that set up time-sharing networks for use by their own widely dispersed employees. Keydata's was the first service to bring the enormous promise of data-processing technology to workaday businesses that could not afford their own computers. "Ours," said Keydata's president at the time, Jack Gilmore, "is an honest-to-God, meat-and-potatoes business for businessmen."

So-called terminal-oriented systems such as Keydata's were an important early stage in the evolution of new ways to link computers into networks. In these schemes, a host computer serves a multitude of terminals connected to it through the telephone system. Each can communicate with the host but not with another terminal. Later, more elaborate networks emerged to make possible a dialogue among several host computers. Distant computers could use one another's specialized software and files of valuable information, such as programs in a computer at M.I.T. for finding solutions to mathematical equations so complex that some had never been worked out manually.

One major obstacle stood in the way of these advances — incompatibility among computers. As a rule, the operating codes of machines from different manufacturers, like the speech of people from different countries, are mutually unintelligible. For example, one computer may express letters and numbers in a different code from another. Or one machine may transmit data at a rate that another is unprepared to accept. For networks to advance, they had to compensate for such variations, and they did so with increasingly elaborate sets of rules known in the trade as protocols.

The term comes from the world of diplomacy, where it refers to the formalities vital to ensuring that heads of state do not unwittingly give offense because of cultural differences. Computer protocols describe in fine detail precisely the form that data must take before it can pass through a network, the rate at which host computers may transmit information and how data is to be checked for errors that might occur en route, to name just a few of the issues that such rules address. Properly observed, protocols allow different kinds and brands of computer equipment to converse in a common language.

A WELCOME ALTERNATIVE TO BATCH PROCESSING

It was fitting that the first time-sharing network for businesses was centered in Cambridge. Most of the early research into time sharing was accomplished there, at M.I.T. Work began in 1959, after John McCarthy, cofounder of M.I.T.'s artificial-intelligence laboratory, wrote a memo to his colleagues spelling out how time sharing might be implemented. McCarthy had been prodded into action by his long-standing frustration over batch processing, the way most computers of the day did their work. This cumbersome system compelled anyone seeking use of the machine to hand over to a computer operator a batch of cards punched with holes that coded the program to be run or the problem to be solved. The operator fed the cards into the computer for processing, one batch at a time. Depending on the length of the queue and the complexity of the programs and problems, it was not unusual to wait 24 hours or more for results.

McCarthy may have been the impetus behind time sharing at M.I.T., but others attended to the details. In 1961, a team of programmers headed by McCarthy's colleague Fernando J. Corbató demonstrated the feasibility of the time-sharing concept by writing software that converted an IBM 709 mainframe computer into a host for multiple terminals. Further progress was made at M.I.T. by scientists associated with Project MAC, funded by the Advanced Research Projects Agency (ARPA) of the U.S. Department of Defense. MAC was an unusual acronym in that it had a double meaning: Multi-Access Computer and Machine-Aided Cognition. ARPA's business was to foster new technologies that might be useful to the military, directly or indirectly. With three million dollars annually from ARPA, the project grew into a tool that eventually gave scientists as far away as Norway access to a powerful computer. Though not personally involved in time sharing after his memo started the ball rolling, McCarthy was a catalyst who became, in the words of Gwen Bell, curator of the Computer Museum in Boston, computer time sharing's "visionary spokesperson." At a symposium marking M.I.T.'s 1961 centennial celebration, he conjectured that computing "may someday be organized as a public utility, just as the telephone system is a public utility. We can envisage computing service companies whose subscribers are connected to them by telephone lines. Each subscriber needs to pay only for the capacity that he actually uses, but he has access to all programming languages characteristic of a very large system."

DARTMOUTH'S CONTRIBUTION

An early step in that direction was a time-sharing system put together in 1964 at Dartmouth College, where 24 years earlier, Bell Telephone's George Stibitz had staged the world's first demonstration of telecomputing with his Complex Number Calculator. The Dartmouth system, a local network designed by students and faculty for teaching computer science, utilized two computers. One carried out the actual processing, while a smaller computer acted as a kind of traffic cop, routing requests from network terminals for slices of processing time. Other campuses soon began to buy time on the Dartmouth network, which by 1967 could accommodate dozens of terminals operating concurrently.

The two Dartmouth professors who spearheaded the design of the system, John Kemeny and Thomas Kurtz, saw time sharing as a milestone in the democratization of computing. "Up to now the public has been hoodwinked by computer professionals," said Kurtz in 1967. "The customer was at the mercy of the computer and its staff, and was very happy to get any computing time. Now you are putting the computer in the hands of the customer; now the computer is in the marketplace for the first time."

Soon after the inauguration of the Dartmouth network, General Electric, which had supplied the computers to run the system, marketed a commercial adapta-

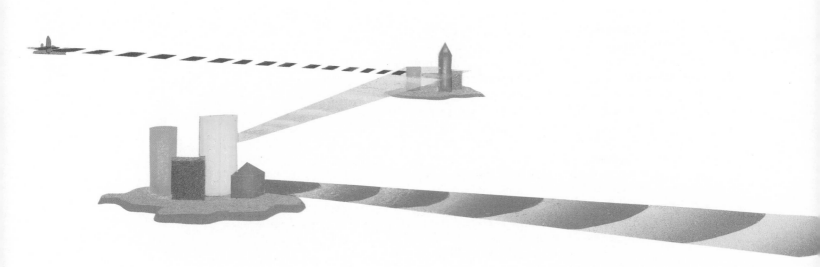

tion of the Dartmouth time-sharing software. Then, after Keydata and other small service companies plunged into the business, GE launched its own time-sharing network, based on the Dartmouth model. By 1968, GE had built commercial networks serving 50,000 customers from 31 time-sharing centers.

The colossus of the computer industry, IBM, lagged behind the competition in developing time-sharing hardware and software all through the 1960s. But practically every other manufacturer followed GE's lead and jumped in to provide time-sharing computers and programs for what was rapidly becoming a hot new business opportunity.

The economics of time-sharing networks were such that consumers and network suppliers alike came out ahead. A retailer tracking inventory or a manufacturer making out a payroll, for example, could connect a terminal to a time-sharing network for about $10 per hour, whereas an exclusive lease of the equipment might raise the cost as high as $140 per hour. A network supplier could acquire a host computer for about $20,000 a month with the expectation of bringing in five times that amount in revenues.

By the late 1960s, new commercial networks were being formed at the rate of three or four a month — and with Wall Street's enthusiastic blessing. One young entrepreneur described the atmosphere this way: "All you have to do is get a few good guys and yell 'Time sharing!' and they bury you up to your neck in money. Then you rent a computer, and you're in business."

However, many network operators found themselves with unexpected difficulties. Computer circuits and phone lines were fickle, and even a slight waver in the electric power could wipe out all of a customer's data stored temporarily in the machine's memory. And customers balked at long-distance telephone charges that often exceeded the cost of time sharing itself. Only the biggest of the vendors, such as General Electric, could afford to alleviate the burden of long-distance tolls by sprinkling host computers around the nation to allow most customers to make dial-up connections with a local telephone call.

ROUND TRIP TO KANSAS CITY, PLEASE

General-purpose networks such as those established by Dartmouth and General Electric permitted clients to use the service for any task they were clever enough to make it perform. For example, John Van Geen, who perfected the portable modem *(page 20),* used the computer at Dartmouth to perform the calculations necessary for his analyses of the physics of shock waves. But a second category of terminal-oriented network, dedicated to a single purpose such as handling airline reservations or providing up-to-the-minute quotations of prices on major stock exchanges, also began to flourish during the 1960s. The most notable of the early special-purpose networks was a reservation system named Semi-Automated Business Research Environment. Better known as SABRE, it was developed by IBM for American Airlines and was later adopted by other airlines.

SABRE became fully operational about the same time as Dartmouth's time-sharing system. With some 2,000 terminals across the U.S. connected by 12,000 miles of leased telephone lines to the host computer in Briarcliff, New York, it was the world's largest commercial real-time network. Each terminal gave a ticket agent access to a central data base containing seat reservations for all of American's many daily flights. The agent could query the computer about space on any flight and make reservations as much as a year in advance. Responding to each request in the then-remarkable time of less than three seconds, the computer automatically updated the inventory of seats available after each reservation or cancellation.

SABRE's speed resulted in part from the use of special high-capacity dedicated telephone lines in sections of the system. Making such a connection between each terminal and the host computer would have been exorbitantly expensive. Instead, electronic storage devices called terminal interchanges were placed between the host and the terminals. Queries traveled from terminals by way of less expensive, lower-capacity dedicated lines to a regional interchange, which stored the messages. A split second later, the central computer, rapidly polling each interchange in turn, ordered the accumulated traffic to be forwarded over the high-capacity circuits. The effect was that of a host computer giving its undivided attention to each terminal.

THE ADVANTAGES OF A SIMPLE WEB
Terminal-oriented networks such as SABRE and the multitude of time-sharing services that emerged during the 1960s would prove to be among the simpler webs spun in computer communications. With only one host computer involved, no questions of authority arose; the host was in charge. Nor was incompatibility among computers much of an issue; a subscriber to a service was supplied with the correct type of terminal and communications equipment. Lack of compatibility among networks posed difficulties only for those who hooked up to more than one of them. A major corporation, for example, might subscribe to as many as four different time-sharing systems, each specializing in a different aspect of data processing, such as engineering problems or inventory control. As a result, it was not unheard of to find one person's office cluttered with terminals for distinct tasks.

Problems of authority and compatibility were greatly magnified when experiments began toward the next stage in the evolution of computer networks: host-to-host communication. With the potential for a variety of powerful computers to be linked by a network, questions arose about which host would speak first and what the arrangements would be for translating their data into a common tongue.

In the mid-1960s, ARPA, the Defense Department agency that had supported early time-sharing research, launched an effort to address these issues. The goal of this ambitious project, which would be known as Arpanet, was to link in a single coast-to-coast network a dozen or more computers of different types located at colleges, laboratories and other institutions engaged in research for the Defense Department.

Arpanet's architect was Lawrence G. Roberts, director for information-processing techniques at ARPA. Before joining the agency in 1967, Roberts had earned his Ph.D. in electrical engineering at M.I.T. He then served as chief of the software group at M.I.T.'s Lincoln Laboratory, where he helped develop systems for three-dimensional graphics input and for time sharing. Even in those early days Roberts was convinced, he wrote later, "that the most important problem in the computer field before us was computer networking: the ability to access one computer from another easily and economically to permit resource sharing."

At ARPA, Roberts found much duplication of effort among agency-funded research centers, especially in the generation of specialized software and data bases. There had to be a way, he decided, to grant investigators at one center access to the research tools and information that investigators at other centers had already developed.

ROUTING BURSTS OF DATA

From experiments Roberts had conducted at Lincoln Laboratory, he had already come to the conclusion that the telephone system's technique for handling ordinary phone calls as well as computer data—a method of routing known as circuit switching—was inappropriate for the network he envisioned. Although well adapted to steady streams of computer data, such as the uninterrupted transmission of banking-transaction records that are millions of bits long, circuit switching is far from ideal for applications that produce data of a "bursty" nature.

For example, an engineer might send a computer a problem to solve, then wait a short while for the answer. The cumulative cost of a circuit during such periods of idleness can quickly become a burden. Furthermore, circuit switching establishes a communications path at the beginning of a transmission and breaks the circuit only after all the data has been transferred. Others are denied use of the circuit during the idle moments.

To replace circuit switching, Roberts selected a new and untried technology that would permit several computers to use a circuit concurrently. The idea was first published in a study of digital communications carried out by the Rand Corporation for the U.S. Air Force during the early 1960s. The author of the study, a brilliant computer communications specialist named Paul Baran, had been given the challenge of creating a secure telephone network—one that resisted wire tapping, for example, and that would be able to survive extensive damage in an enemy attack.

Baran's ingenious solution was first to digitize the information that was to be transmitted, converting it from an analog signal to a digital one, then to equip each junction, or node, of the network with a small, high-speed computer. The computers nearest the participants in a conversation would chop the outgoing portions into small segments and then transmit them by way of the computers at intervening nodes. En route, the message segments would be mixed with segments of other conversations. An electronic eavesdropper would detect only the garble from dozens of conversations. The computer at the node nearest the destination would reassemble the scrambled pieces into intelligible order and reconstruct the conversation. Because control of the network was to be distributed among all the computers and because there were many possible routes by which a chunk of data might reach its destination, the system could survive even if many parts were lost to bombing or sabotage.

Baran completed his study in 1964, but it became entangled in bureaucratic maneuvering within the Department of Defense. A British researcher named Donald Davies, working independently in the United Kingdom on a similar concept, later gave a name to Baran's message segments. He called them packets and coined a name for the technique of transmitting them: packet switching.

Roberts recognized that packet switching was the perfect solution for Arpanet. Serendipitously, a new, more modest class of computers had emerged. Called minicomputers, they were just the right size to take on tasks like packet switching that were too small for mainframes to tackle economically.

RESCUING A CONCEPT FROM OBSCURITY
Despite the apparent advantages of packet switching, Roberts ran into a wall of skepticism and even of hostility when he attempted to discuss his proposal with professionals in the communications field. "Everybody thought I was crazy," he recalled. "People actually would hoot and scream at the meetings. They didn't think it would work, and they got violently angry. They had their lives invested in

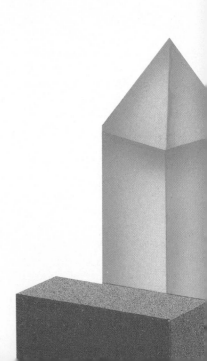

the old technology and couldn't change their minds. We were talking about a new way of doing business, and they couldn't accept it." Such hostility between the worlds of computers and communications was commonplace in those days. Computer people wanted to apply their new technology to the telephone system, but Bell engineers were particularly wedded to tradition and distrustful of new schemes that originated outside their own, highly proficient research labs.

And the Arpanet scheme was certainly radical. As conceived by Roberts and designed by Bolt Beranek and Newman Inc., the Cambridge firm that won the contract to build and operate the network, Arpanet actually consisted of two levels of computers. On one level were the big host computers, such as the ILLIAC IV and the IBM 360/91, being tied together by the network. On the other level stood minicomputers — Honeywell H-516s and H-316s, for example — whose role was to facilitate communication among the hosts.

These network computers, called interface message processors, or IMPs, were responsible for two major tasks. One was to link host computers — which could in fact be either minicomputers or mainframes — to the network. Essential to making this connection was a combination of hardware and software, custom-tailored to each host, that applied common coding and control procedures to each computer's data and slowed or accelerated the flow of bits as necessary to match the network's transmission rate. The second task was to serve as a switching center for moving along the packets of data. Later, a special kind of IMP known as a terminal interface processor, or TIP, was added to allow terminals without host computers to connect to Arpanet and select among all the hosts in the network. An IMP can support up to four host computers; a TIP can handle as many as 63 different terminals.

Traffic flow in Arpanet begins when data zips through a cable from a host computer to an IMP switching node. The IMP disassembles each message into packets and attaches the recipient's network address to each one. Then, by a packet-routing scheme called the datagram method (pages 72-73), each packet is passed from one network IMP computer to another until it reaches the IMP that serves the host computer to which the message is directed. When all the packets of a message have arrived, the IMP reassembles them in the correct sequence and sends them on to the host, which in turn displays the results on the appropriate terminal. All this activity occurs in a twinkling over high-capacity leased lines capable of carrying 50,000 bits per second. The host-to-host transmission time for a packet averages less than half a second. In that time, a packet may travel from the Atlantic coast to the Pacific.

A SMASHING SUCCESS

When Arpanet went on-line late in 1969, it linked only three West Coast research centers and the University of Utah. In less than two years, however, the network expanded to some 15 minicomputer nodes scattered across the country. And during the next decade the network burgeoned to embrace nearly 100 nodes, including satellite links to centers in Hawaii, Great Britain and even Scandinavia, that served more than 400 host computers and a user community of some 10,000 people.

As Roberts had foreseen, resource sharing played a large role in the daily life of the network. For example, the Stanford Research Institute (now SRI International), awaiting delivery of a computer to help with various research projects, hooked up with a similar machine at the University of Utah to begin developing software for it. A small software company in Massachusetts exploited the three-hour difference in time zones to gain access to a mainframe more than 3,000 miles away, at the University of Southern California, during that machine's off-peak hours. The University of Illinois obtained computer services from four different centers at one third the price of purchasing the computing power locally. By 1973, the increase in productivity gained from resource sharing on Arpanet was more than enough to offset the cost of operating the network, about four million dollars a year.

But there were other, unexpected payoffs as well. Perhaps the most significant was the development of electronic mail *(pages 26-27)*, which made it possible to share ideas almost instantaneously and helped forge a nationwide research community. According to one participant, Keith Uncapher, executive director of the Information Sciences Institute at the University of Southern California, Arpanet "had tremendous impact on the pace of scientific discovery. People began to share results almost day by day instead of week by week or waiting to publish something in a scholarly journal." Researchers who knew of Arpanet but had no access to the network, he said, "felt they were second-class citizens because every discovery was generally put into one computer system and instantly made available to all others on the network." On some projects, Uncapher recalled, the give-and-take was so extensive that it was often difficult to pin down precisely who deserved credit as the author of a particular scientific paper.

PACKET SWITCHING GOES PUBLIC

In the early 1970s, while Arpanet was still in its infancy, the network's phenomenal takeoff led Larry Roberts to envision a commercial offspring. Arpanet was restricted to projects sponsored by the Defense Department or of special interest to it. Looking beyond this limited horizon, Roberts discerned a potentially vast market for a public packet-switched network connecting the dissimilar computers and terminals of all kinds of customers, from colleges to nonmilitary governmental agencies and private industry.

Roberts approached the two telecommunications giants of the day, AT&T and Western Union, which operated the only networks that spanned the nation and thus were the only companies that could provide the service that Roberts had in mind. His reception was as chilly as the one he had encountered a few years earlier when he first proposed the radical notion of packet switching for Arpanet. "Larry talked to both of them," recalled a colleague, "and it was sort of the not-invented-here syndrome. It hadn't come out of Bell Labs, so obviously as far as AT&T was concerned it had no merit. And Western Union still had its green eye shades on from the telegraph days." At least part of AT&T's reaction to Roberts' proposal also sprang from doubts about the future profitability of a public packet-switched service.

One company that shared Roberts' vision was the Cambridge research and engineering firm that had served as principal contractor for Arpanet — Bolt Beranek and Newman. Late in 1972, the firm established a subsidiary, Telenet Communications Corporation, to set up a commercial packet-switching network, and the following year Roberts was hired as president of the company.

Licensed by the Federal Communications Commission as a common carrier —
a company selling communications or transportation services to the public —
Telenet inaugurated service to seven cities in 1975. A decade later — by which
time it was a subsidiary of the telecommunications giant GTE (formerly General
Telephone and Electronics) — Telenet had far outstripped Arpanet. Serving more
than half a million terminal users in and around 400 U.S. cities, GTE Telenet also
linked about 1,500 host computers and provided connections to data networks in
more than 50 other nations. The network's services ranged the communications
gamut, from electronic mail and access to commercial data bases to processing point-of-sale transactions for merchants. Telenet grew so rapidly that all
its potential profits went toward expanding the network, delaying profitability
until 1983 and in part confirming AT&T's misgivings about the project's
money-making potential.

Though Telenet borrowed heavily from the technology of Arpanet, it also
differed significantly from its precursor. As a money-saving measure, for example, Telenet modified Arpanet's method of routing packets to their destinations.
Instead of choosing the least-congested route for each packet (pages 74-75),
Telenet selected a speedy route for the first packet of a message, then forwarded
the remaining packets along the same path. Doing so reduced the number of
telephone circuits used by the network, a measure that resulted in lower costs.

ADDING VALUE

Telenet, the first public packet-switched network, was followed during the 1970s
by similar services in Great Britain, Japan, Canada and France. France's
Transpac serves as the network for the transmission of the popular service, Teletel
(pages 7-8). Networks like these are sometimes referred to as VANs — for value-
added networks. Value is said to be added to a network when additional services
supplement the basic one of establishing connections among subscribers. In the
case of packet-switched networks, value is added by the computer switching
centers that provide error checking and compatibility among dissimilar computers and terminals, as well as such services as electronic mail.

With the advent of packet-switching VANs, the boundary between computing
and communicating, once sharply etched, became blurred: Computer technology increasingly helped run the telephone system, and the telephone system was
essential to the operation of many computer networks. The ambiguities were of
more than academic interest in the U.S., for the FCC's regulation of common
carriers hinged largely upon precise definitions of data processing, or computing,
and data communications. In 1966, the FCC launched a formal investigation,
Computer Inquiry I, into the gradual convergence of the two domains. Over the
next two decades, the study would be followed by Computer Inquiry II and
Computer Inquiry III.

The thorny regulatory issues raised by the confusing overlap between computing and communicating were illustrated by the evolution of one of Telenet's
principal competitors, Tymnet. Whereas Telenet began as a communications
network, Tymnet had started out as a terminal-oriented system established to
facilitate the time-sharing business of its parent concern, Tymshare, Inc. Thus,
Tymnet's clear purpose — at least in the beginning — was to provide computer
services to its customers. Communications were an incidental necessity.

But as it turned out, Tymnet had built a network with more capacity than the time-sharing business could fill. To use some of the excess, Tymnet contracted with the National Institutes of Health (NIH) to provide communications links between terminals installed in medical schools and a computer and bibliographic data base belonging to the NIH's National Library of Medicine. This arrangement worked out so well that other host computers were added to the network, which employed a variant of the packet-switching technology pioneered by Arpanet.

Tymnet continued to regard itself as a time-sharing network, even though the company seemed to have entered the business of providing communications facilities for organizations other than Tymshare. This transformation attracted the attention of Telenet officials, who held the opinion that Tymnet should be obliged to operate under the restrictions imposed by FCC regulation. For example, as an FCC-regulated common carrier, Telenet had to publish its rates and stick to them. This restriction made it easy for Tymnet, which could charge any price it pleased, to underbid Telenet in negotiations with potential customers. Accordingly, Telenet filed a complaint with the FCC in 1975, seeking to have Tymnet obtain common-carrier status. The issue evaporated in 1980 when the FCC handed down its findings from Computer Inquiry II, which included a change in policy; VANs such as Telenet and Tymnet would no longer fall under the watchful eye of the FCC. As a result, a number of companies that had been hesitant to enter a regulated industry jumped in to establish networks. Among the new participants was the reluctant giant, AT&T.

NEEDED: A COMMON GROUND FOR COMMUNICATIONS

As networks advanced from terminal-oriented systems to packet-switched, computer-to-computer linkups, the protocols necessary to make networks function also grew more complex. Established during the 1960s even before the advent of packet switching, the first and most fundamental of these protocols addressed the need for a universal code to represent data. This code had to specify how many bits would make up a character and then spell out which patterns of bits—the precise order of ones and zeros—would be assigned to each character. (Characters include not only letters, numbers and punctuation marks but also control commands such as DELETE and BACKSPACE, as well as special communications signals that, for example, mark the beginning and end of a message.)

To a large degree, the structure of a coding system is arbitrary. Each computer maker had its own way of encoding data within its machines, and some builders even had multiple encoding schemes for their various products. In 1960, when the formal search for a standard was launched, IBM counted no fewer than nine different codes in its own diverse line of computers.

Then, as now, the creation and acceptance of even a simple protocol for computers proceeded at a glacial pace. Development of a coding protocol fell to the X3 Committee of the American Standards Association (ASA). The committee—X3 meant the third committee to be formed on the subject of information processing and related technologies—was composed of representatives from government, computer manufacturers and the communications industry. After a four-year effort, the committee in 1964 succeeded in having the 128-character,

Players and Rules in Data Transmission

The worldwide network of data communications hinges on the ability of different brands and models of computers to talk with one another electronically, often over telephone lines. In the United States, a standard known as the RS-232 (RS stands for "recommended standard") specifies the interconnections between computers and telecommunications equipment such as modems. (The standard, with minor variations, has also come to be used for communication between computers and such peripheral machines as printers.)

In the version shown here, known as RS-232-C, a plug that hooks a computer to a modem has 25 pin connections. Some connections are active for the duration of a given communi-

cation; others come into play only for particular types of transmissions. The pins provide channels for the exchange of data in binary code. They also set up so-called handshaking protocols, which establish such details as whether an exchange will be conducted in full or half duplex — that is, whether a computer will be able to transmit and receive simultaneously or must take turns with the other machine. In addition, although the RS-232-C does not prescribe a fixed speed for communications, it does offer a standard range of speeds from which the sending and receiving computers may select the one most suitable for a given application.

The sequence at right depicts the steps required to establish a data-communications link between two computer systems, A and B, beginning with the handshake between sending Terminal A and its modem. (In other modems, other protocols and pins may be involved.) Once all protocols have been established and data transmission begins, the modem's primary function is to convert, or modulate, the sending computer's digital pulses into the telephone system's analog signals, a process that may occur in one of several ways, as described on pages 52-53.

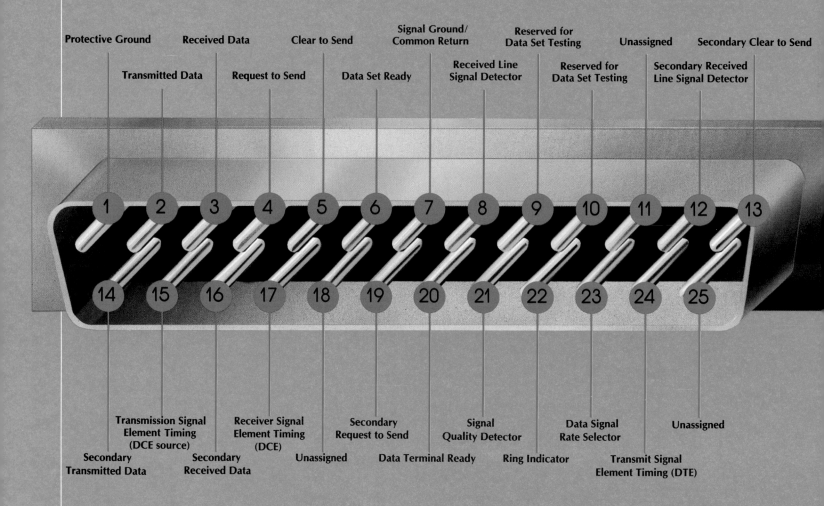

Protective Ground   Received Data   Clear to Send   Signal Ground/Common Return   Reserved for Data Set Testing   Unassigned   Secondary Clear to Send

Transmitted Data   Request to Send   Data Set Ready   Received Line Signal Detector   Reserved for Data Set Testing   Secondary Received Line Signal Detector

Secondary Transmitted Data   Transmission Signal Element Timing (DCE source)   Secondary Received Data   Receiver Signal Element Timing (DCE)   Unassigned   Secondary Request to Send   Data Terminal Ready   Signal Quality Detector   Ring Indicator   Data Signal Rate Selector   Transmit Signal Element Timing (DTE)   Unassigned

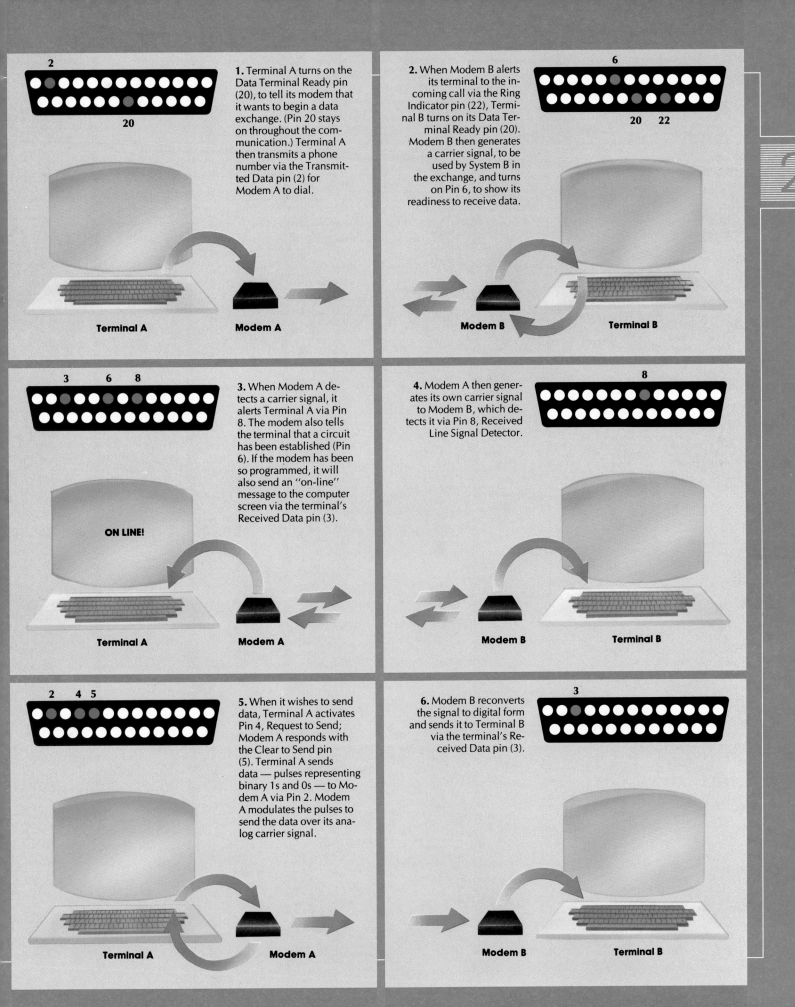

2

20

1. Terminal A turns on the Data Terminal Ready pin (20), to tell its modem that it wants to begin a data exchange. (Pin 20 stays on throughout the communication.) Terminal A then transmits a phone number via the Transmitted Data pin (2) for Modem A to dial.

Terminal A   **Modem A**

---

2. When Modem B alerts its terminal to the incoming call via the Ring Indicator pin (22), Terminal B turns on its Data Terminal Ready pin (20). Modem B then generates a carrier signal, to be used by System B in the exchange, and turns on Pin 6, to show its readiness to receive data.

6

20   22

Modem B   **Terminal B**

---

3   6   8

3. When Modem A detects a carrier signal, it alerts Terminal A via Pin 8. The modem also tells the terminal that a circuit has been established (Pin 6). If the modem has been so programmed, it will also send an "on-line" message to the computer screen via the terminal's Received Data pin (3).

ON LINE!

Terminal A   **Modem A**

---

4. Modem A then generates its own carrier signal to Modem B, which detects it via Pin 8, Received Line Signal Detector.

8

Modem B   **Terminal B**

---

2   4   5

5. When it wishes to send data, Terminal A activates Pin 4, Request to Send; Modem A responds with the Clear to Send pin (5). Terminal A sends data — pulses representing binary 1s and 0s — to Modem A via Pin 2. Modem A modulates the pulses to send the data over its analog carrier signal.

Terminal A   **Modem A**

---

6. Modem B reconverts the signal to digital form and sends it to Terminal B via the terminal's Received Data pin (3).

3

Modem B   **Terminal B**

Modulating a Signal to Convey a Message

The message sent by a modem holds not only digital computer data converted to analog form, but control information that helps the receiver sample the transmission at correct intervals. Two methods for encoding data onto an analog carrier wave are frequency-shift keying (FSK) and differential phase-shift keying (DPSK). Both change a given characteristic of the carrier. Each individual change is known as a baud. With FSK, the modem varies the wave's frequency *(bottom)*, a method that limits transmission to 1,800 bits per second (bps); higher speeds would require a wider bandwidth than that supplied by the telephone voice channel. With DPSK, higher transmission rates are possible — 2,400 and 4,800 bps are common. DPSK varies the phase of the carrier wave *(right)* and encodes two bits (known as a dibit) with each shift.

Before a communications circuit is established, the sending and receiving systems must be compatible on two related issues in order to be mutually intelligible. First, the systems must transmit and receive data at the same rate. If the sending rate is 1,200 bits per second, for example, the receiving modem must sample the incoming signal every $\frac{1}{1,200}$ of a second, converting the result into either a zero or a one. Second, the receiving modem needs a synchronizing marker, called a start bit, to know precisely when to begin sampling. In so-called asynchronous transmission *(below)*, the sending modem supplies a start bit with each small group of data bits. (For example, the American Standard Code for Information Interchange, or ASCII, uses seven bits to encode characters and spaces.) The receiving modem thus resynchronizes its sampling rate with the transmission rate fairly often, reducing chances that errors will have a cumulative effect on the message. This slows transmission, however. In synchronous mode, by contrast, the modem begins sampling when it first detects the carrier signal and resynchronizes periodically, after much larger blocks of data. This allows high transmission rates but requires extremely accurate clocks in both modems to ensure synchronization and to avoid cumulative errors.

A Matter of Control and Proper Timing

In a typical asynchronous transmission, an ASCII string is bracketed by control bits: a start bit *(far right)* that tells the modem to begin sampling the signal at the agreed-upon rate; an optional bit that is sometimes used as a so-called parity, or error, check; and a stop bit that tells the modem to resynchronize its clock at the next start bit.

Sending Zeros and Ones on Different Frequencies

The two pairs of frequencies at right are characteristic of modems that transmit at 300 bps, using frequency-shift keying in full-duplex mode (sending and receiving at the same time). Operating within the 4,000 hertz allocated for the telephone voice channel, the modem that originates the session transmits data by generating a carrier wave at either 1,070 hertz (for 0s) or 1,270 hertz (for 1s). Its counterpart transmits 0s at 2,025 hertz and 1s at 2,225 hertz. With FSK, only one bit is encoded per frequency shift.

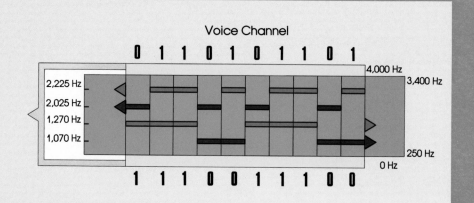

The Power of Shifting Phases

A modem employing differential phase-shift keying can encode eight or more bits of data — at two bits (one dibit) per shift — on one frequency, compared with the single bit per frequency change of the FSK method. This is accomplished by manipulating the phase of the carrier wave. As shown in the graph below, a wave's cycle may be measured from peak to peak, from zero point to zero point or from trough to trough. A cycle may be divided into phases, or points, typically expressed in terms of degrees. For example, 0° represents the starting point of the cycle, 90° the one-quarter point, 180° the halfway point and so on.

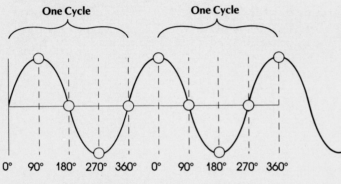

In the DPSK method shown at right, a carrier may, in effect, be split into four waves, each with the frequency of the original but starting at a different phase of the original cycle. Four phases can represent all possible combinations of two bits; the modem merely chooses the appropriate phase shift for the dibit to be encoded (table, below). The shift is always calculated in relation to the starting point of the previous cycle. For example, if the previous cycle began at a peak (blue), a 180° shift to encode the dibit 11 would jump two phases to start at a trough (orange).

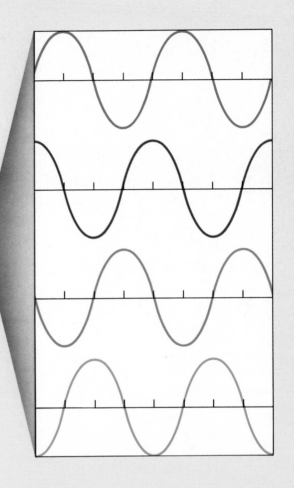

Dibit Table	
To encode	requires a shift of
00	0°
01	90°
11	180°
10	270°

Binary Coding by Phase Shift

To encode a series of dibits, some modems first generate two complete cycles, measured from the zero line (red). At the end of the second cycle, a 90° shift (blue) is made to encode the first dibit (01). Encoding another 01 produces a wave cycle (green) that represents a one-phase shift from the blue cycle. The next shift, to encode the dibit 11, jumps 180°, or two phases, from the green cycle to the red one, and so on. After each shift, two full cycles are completed to confirm the new starting point.

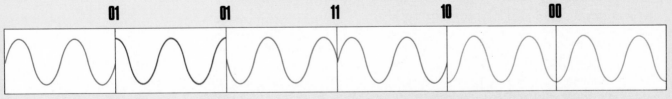

seven-bit pattern known as ASCII adopted as the new standard. ASCII, which rhymes with "passkey," stands for American Standard Code for Information Interchange. Two more years elapsed before the International Organization for Standardization, of which ASA was a member, adopted ASCII for worldwide use.

Partly responsible for the delay in promulgating ASCII was IBM. Although the company had been the prime mover in the search for a standard, it opposed the adoption of seven-bit ASCII, favoring instead its own data-encoding scheme, known as EBCDIC (Extended Binary Coded Decimal Interchange Code) — and with good reason. EBCDIC's eight bits could represent twice as many characters as ASCII's seven-bit pattern. Moreover, much was at stake for IBM. Had EBCDIC been adopted by ASA, the company's computers, without modification, would have been at least somewhat ready for communicating with other computers. As things turned out, IBM was forced into the expense of providing internal mechanisms to translate EBCDIC to ASCII for purposes of external communications.

With ASCII established as the common method of coding data for communications, another kind of protocol was needed to specify precisely how the encoded information would be transmitted by modem over a telephone wire. To lay down procedures for the link between computer and modem, a protocol was issued in 1969 by a coalition of interested groups: the Electronics Industries Association, various manufacturers of communications equipment and Bell Laboratories. Named RS-232-C (RS means "recommended standard"), it covers virtually all aspects of the modem-computer dialogue. For example, RS-232-C specifies voltage levels for signals exchanged between the two devices. It also defines the number of wires in the cable — 25 — and assigns a function to each of them and to the pins that link them in the connector *(pages 50-51)*.

RAISING THE PROTOCOL ANTE
ASCII and RS-232-C were easy to implement compared to the difficulty of satisfying the additional demands for compatibility made by packet-switched, computer-to-computer networks such as Arpanet. The protocols to do so were almost unimaginably complex, controlling as they did such matters as the physical and electrical connections between host computers and the network, error detection and the procedures for packet formatting and routing. Formulating, testing and revising a set of these rules accounted for much of the time consumed in achieving a functioning network.

To complicate matters further, with each new network there appeared a different set of protocols. Invariably, each network's set of protocols was unique, if only subtly so. Telenet's experience typified the problem. It had formulated a protocol for connecting host computers to the network. This protocol, which borrowed a broad set of capabilities from Arpanet and from some networking ideas developed at IBM, required custom software but no special hardware. Stu Mathison, one of Telenet's founders, recalled that most customers laughed when they saw the 100 pages of specifications that needed to be implemented at the customer's expense to hook into the network. "And when we went to the computer manufacturers and said would you implement this on behalf of all your customers," they too balked at the expense.

In 1974 the matter of standardizing the mating between computers and packet-switching networks was taken up by an international organization, the CCITT, the French acronym for International Telegraph and Telephone Consultative Committee. The Geneva-based CCITT is a branch of the International Telecommunications Union, which in turn is an arm of the United Nations. Pressure to establish a world-standard protocol came not only from the obvious need for one but from another source as well: IBM had recently announced a networking scheme, Systems Network Architecture (SNA), intended to link together its own computers.

This development sounded an alarm among some foresighted individuals in the packet-switching business. David Horton was one of them. At the time, Horton worked for the Canadian telephone company. He and representatives of France's Transpac and the United Kingdom's post office, which was in charge of the telephone system, decided that it was imperative "to ward off IBM," as Horton recalled. "If IBM ran rampant with its own protocols, eventually everyone would have to follow IBM standards."

A QUADRENNIAL CHALLENGE
CCITT meetings at which protocols can be adopted occur only once every four years. The wheels of the CCITT grind exceedingly slowly, and though the next meeting was two years away, old hands at the commission doubted that any measure could be guided through the bureaucracy in such a short time. IBM was equally certain that the CCITT could not publish a protocol before SNA ruled the communications roost. At a 1974 meeting of IBM and telephone-company officials dealing with communications issues, Horton announced his and others' intention to push a protocol through CCITT at the earliest opportunity. In response, remembered Horton, a "senior IBM executive said: 'You guys will spend the next four years deciding when you're going to have a meeting, and it's going to be ten years before you have a standard.' " IBM had thrown down the gauntlet; Horton and the others picked it up.

They had something of a head start. Earlier, Horton and his Canadian colleagues had worked up a proposal for a packet-switching protocol, published it on glossy paper and sent it to computer companies, consumers and providers of data transmission services, and to others interested in the subject. The recipients had responded with suggestions for improving the proposed protocol.

Realizing that an American presence might help speed the proposal through CCITT, Horton and his French and British colleagues recruited Telenet for the role. There followed 18 hectic months of travel to meetings in Geneva, Ottawa, Tokyo, Paris and London. During sessions that sometimes lasted well into the night, Horton's group cajoled engineers into pinning down the endless technical details that would make the protocol work and maneuvered politically to keep the project from being derailed. For example, on the eve of the CCITT meeting in 1976 to consider approving the standard, those opposing it attempted to strike the measure from the agenda on the grounds that French and Spanish translations were not available.

That thrust was parried as an inconsequential technicality that had been violated on other occasions, and by the time the final gavel closed the proceedings in Geneva at 5:09 p.m. on March 2, 1976, a new international packet-switching protocol, called X.25, had been approved. "It was a very draining exercise, I can tell you," said Horton. "We all breathed a great sigh of relief and went out and had a hell of a party that night."

The widespread adoption of X.25 opened the door for the growth of packet-switching networks in the U.S. and abroad. Computer manufacturers began to implement the protocol as a feature in their systems, making it a simple matter to plug any machine using the X.25 standard into a packet-switching network. X.25 led also to several other international protocols, including X.75, which provides for interconnections called gateways between networks of different nations. And it paved the way for the International Organization of Standardization, working closely with CCITT, to formulate in 1978 its reference model for Open Systems Interconnection (OSI) — a seven-layer framework of protocols for data communication *(pages 105-121)*.

NETWORKING FOR THE MASSES

Just as the CCITT seal of approval on the X.25 and X.75 protocols redefined the scope of packet-switched networking in the 1970s, the proliferation of the personal computer during the 1980s broadened the appeal of this technology and helped accelerate its expansion. This democratization of telecomputing also contributed to a degree of confusion in terminology. Among personal-computer enthusiasts, for example, the meaning of the word "network" has come to embrace a broad range of computer communications. In this context, the term refers not only to common carriers such as Telenet and Tymnet but to a multitude of different systems and utilities linked by them: commercial data bases and information services such as The Source and CompuServe, teleconferencing systems, electronic bulletin boards and services such as France's Teletel. For example, a subscriber to The Source may gain access to its computers through Telenet, connecting to the data-base network by means of a telephone call to the local Telenet switching center. A CompuServe customer may hook up by way of Tymnet or through CompuServe's own value-added network.

Every time a personal computer is connected to one of these networks, it serves a dual role. Part of the time it imitates a dumb terminal, acting like an appendage to a time-sharing computer. In this mode, the operator can send messages to the host only by typing them at the keyboard. Although information received from the host can be read on the computer screen or printed, it cannot be stored within the computer. With the proper software, however, the operator can restore the machine's file-management capabilities. Doing so allows the computer to retain messages from the host for future reference and permits information from a word-processing or data-base program to be sent to the host without retyping.

Increasingly sophisticated software has simplified the use of computer networks. For example, improved communications programs working in concert with so-called intelligent modems can, on command, dial a number stored in a computerized telephone directory and automatically redial if the line is busy. Some programs can remember the elaborate procedures required to log on to a network — which typically involve typing a sequence of commands, as well as the subscriber's name and password — and then perform the routine automatically when commanded to do so by a keystroke or two.

But even the best of communications software is all too often frustrating for the beginner, requiring more concentration on the medium than on the message. For example, when a user establishes communications with a service never before dialed up, certain settings must be checked and perhaps adjusted. These settings relate to such matters as speed of transmission, the method used to check a message for errors and whether the connection will occur in full duplex (transmission in both directions simultaneously) or half duplex (in one direction at a time). A seemingly minor mistake can lead to garbled communication — or to no communication at all. And even with the proper settings, a message may be lost for other reasons. Perhaps a letter or other document to be transferred has not been formatted in precisely the manner prescribed by the network. The absence of a few special characters at the beginning or end of a message may lead to the mysterious disappearance of the message after it seemed to have arrived safely at its destination.

Once the technical difficulties are overcome, however, many computer novices become enthusiastic networkers. Some spend so much time on-line that they develop a dependency that social scientists have likened to an addiction. Symptoms include reliance on networking not only for earning a living but also for recreation. Networkers can find virtually anything on-line, including a kind of spiritual fulfillment. Participants on the New Jersey-based Electronic Information and Exchange System can join in electronic meditation by typing +ATTUNE and pressing the RETURN key, whereupon a series of messages intended to calm the spirit and quiet the mind comes to the screen. "Close your eyes, pause quietly for a few moments and be here now," ends the session. "Press RETURN when you feel attuned."

AT THE LOCAL LEVEL
As VANs proliferated during the 1970s, it was perhaps inevitable that someone would apply similar communications principles to networking on a smaller scale, to span corridors within buildings or the streets between buildings rather than continents and oceans. The impetus for such a network was identical to the reason behind Arpanet: the desire to share computer resources. By connecting all the computers and peripheral devices in a headquarters building, an organization could provide wide access to a valuable data base or maximize the productivity of an expensive printer or data-storage unit. Theoretically, it would be possible to establish such a network through Telenet or one of the other VANs, but the cost would be prohibitive. The solution was another kind of network, known as a LAN — for local area network.

The oldest and most prominent of the LANs is Ethernet, a system originally designed in 1973 for minicomputers at Xerox Corporation's Palo Alto Research Center (PARC) in California. Ethernet was the brainchild of a Brooklyn-born computer specialist, Robert Metcalfe, then 27 and self-described as "Type-A aggressive, overcompetitive." At M.I.T., Metcalfe had shouldered a full load of courses, worked as a computer programmer eight hours a night and served as captain of the tennis team. He became immersed in packet-switching technology at M.I.T.; then, while a graduate student at Harvard, he shared responsibility for connecting M.I.T.'s computers to Arpanet.

Metcalfe's Ethernet was inspired largely by Alohanet, a packet-switching network developed by the University of Hawaii to connect, by means of radio transmissions, a central computer with terminals scattered around the

The Local Sharing of Resources and Data

As more and more computers take up residence in the workplace, internal networking systems have become a necessity. Local area networks (LANs) offer efficient communications between personal computers, minicomputers, mainframes and peripherals within a limited geographic area — a building or complex of buildings. LANs not only allow the exchange of information between otherwise isolated computer workstations, they also permit the sharing of such expensive computer resources as large-scale data banks and high-speed laser printers. Because workstations in a LAN-based system are

Taking Turns on the Bus

The bus topology's main thoroughfare is usually a length of coaxial cable — an insulated conductor that carries data in the form of electrical pulses. Each station hooks onto the cable through a transceiver, which sends and receives data and monitors transmissions on the bus. All messages are broadcasted to the entire network, traveling from the sender in both directions along the cable.

When an access-control method called carrier-sense multiple access (CSMA) is used, any station may transmit as soon as it detects no carriers, or message-bearing signals, on the bus. At right, Station A has sensed no traffic and sends a message to Station D. The message begins with the addresses of its destination and its source, and ends with a sequence of bits that Station D will use to check the integrity of the body of the message. Network software and a hardware controller at Station D confirm the message's destination before letting the station accept it.

When more than one station at a time tries to transmit, collisions occur and messages are blocked. The standard CSMA method includes a strategy (opposite) for detecting collisions quickly and clearing the way for retransmission. But because the unpredictable delays caused by such collisions make CSMA inefficient when traffic is steady and heavy, many buses employ a so-called token (page 60, top left) to regulate access.

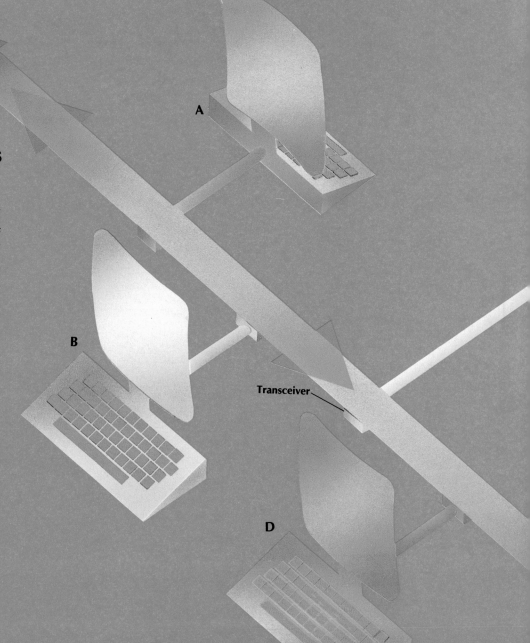

A

B

Transceiver

D

full-fledged computers, each can perform its own processing chores rather than relying on a central mainframe. If one computer malfunctions or is temporarily taken off-line for upgrades in hardware or software, the work of other users on the network most often need not be disrupted.

LANs come in three basic configurations, or topologies, shown here and on the following two pages. Like communications networks generally, local area networks sidestep the complexity and expense of making multiple station-to-station connections by giving each station access to a common transmitting medium — the actual wires, cables or optical fibers that carry data. In a bus topology (below), stations send and receive messages over a central cable. Bus networks generally employ multiple access, which allows any station to transmit when the medium is free. A popular design, the bus is well suited to most office applications. Stations in ring topologies (page 60) connect directly with neighboring stations to form a closed loop. Of particular value in computer-aided manufacturing, rings allow access to be controlled in a more orderly fashion: Data traffic flows smoothly and steadily from station to station on the ring.

The star topology (page 61), similar to the telephone system, uses circuit switching to regulate access through a central station. Though somewhat slower than a bus or ring, it has the advantage of being easily wed to an existing voice network, such as a private branch exchange (PBX), so that voice and data transmissions can travel over the same circuitry. Stars can also be connected with outgoing telephone lines — a preview of the day when all communications services will be integrated in a single digital network.

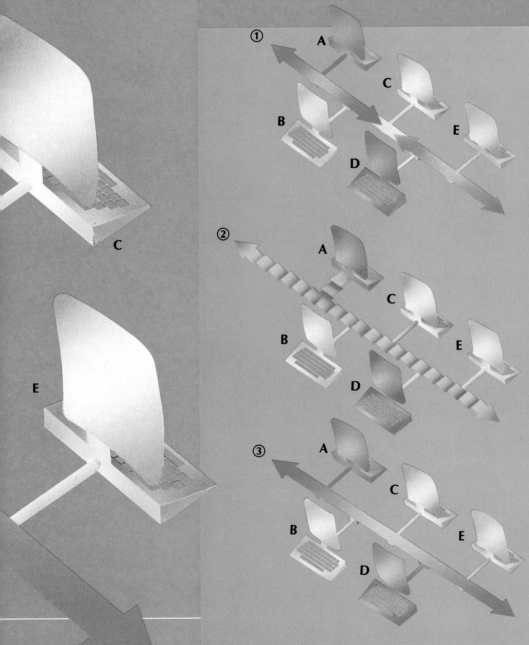

Listening for Collisions

Collisions occur when two or more stations transmit simultaneously or when one station, having not yet detected another's transmission, thinks the bus is free. At left (1), Station A (red) begins sending a message to Station D just as Station E (purple) starts sending to Station B. The sooner these stations detect the impending collision, the less transmission time they will waste. With the collision-detection technique shown here, stations monitor the cable even as they transmit, on the alert for the telltale static of a collision. Here, Station A has detected the collision first and immediately jams the entire bus with a special signal (2), signifying that the line is blocked; A and E consequently abort their transmissions. The jamming noise and the data "wreckage" from the collision are turned into heat and dissipated by resistors at either end of the cable (as is also the case with normal transmissions). In theory, both stations could retransmit as soon as they sense an idle bus, but to avoid another collision, the hardware controller at each station delays retransmission for a random period. Having received a shorter waiting time, A retransmits first and gets its message to D (3), while E waits for the line to clear. Had both stations received the same waiting period — or had other stations also wished to transmit — more collisions would have occurred. Typically, a station will keep trying, informing the user that the network is too busy only after 16 collisions.

The Token Ring

A ring topology uses wire, cable or optical fiber to connect repeating devices at each station into a loop. A repeater, like a bus's transceiver, sends and receives messages; it also regenerates message data — passing it on, bit by bit, to the next station; each station thereby helps maintain the integrity of the data and the signal's strength.

In a token-ring system, a station gains exclusive access to the ring by grabbing and altering the token — usually an eight-bit string — as it circulates on the loop. In the example at right, Station A, with a message for C, has altered the token *(green)* and attached its message *(red)*. Now acting as a message indicator, the token continues on its way, message in tow. The entire transmission is regenerated as it passes through Station B. Station C, finding its address at the head of the message, will copy the data and then, like B, regenerate it onto the ring. When the transmission gets back to the sender, A will remove it, then generate a new token, which B — waiting its turn — is now free to use.

The Slotted Ring

Unlike buses and token rings, slotted rings let more than one station use the network at a time, by circulating not one token but a series of fixed-length slots. Stations divide their messages into slot-size packets, inserting the initial packet in the first empty slot that passes. (A bit at the beginning of each slot marks it as either empty or full.) At right, Station A has already filled a slot *(red)* addressed to Station C, having first changed the lead bit — from 0 to 1, say — to mark it as full; D is also slotting a packet *(purple)* for B. When A's slot reaches C, that station will copy the data into memory and await the rest of A's message. The filled slot will continue around the ring, being regenerated at each station, until it reaches A again, which will change the slot's marker bit back to empty. The next station to use the slot will insert new data, automatically replacing, or overwriting, the old. Only after freeing a slot is A permitted to continue its message — by loading its next packet into the next available slot.

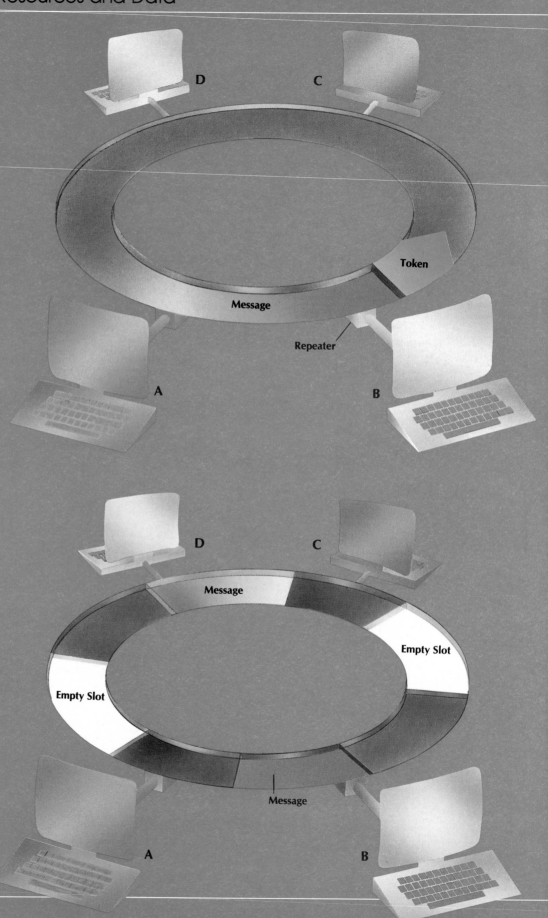

The Star

By centralizing control in a circuit-switching station *(blue)*, the star topology frees individual stations of the many responsibilities that go with distributed access control. Despite some complexity within the central switch, stars are relatively simple, inexpensive setups: They normally use twisted-pair copper wire — ordinary telephone cord — to hook stations into the network. Time-division switching *(box, below)* channels transmissions from different stations, as well as transmissions of different types — voice and data — through the same circuitry. In this example, Station A sends a message to D, and C sends to B; the central switch has established communications pathways for both transmitting stations.

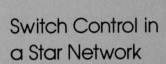

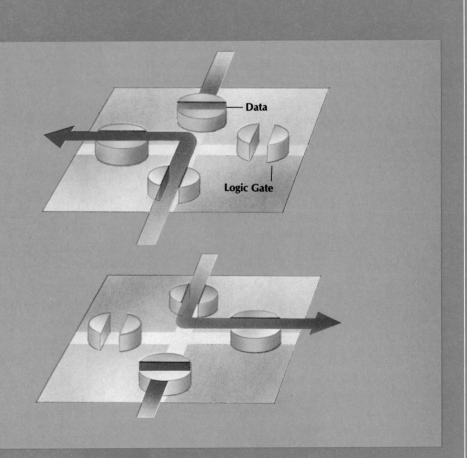

Switch Control in a Star Network

Time-division switching — the star's technique for getting messages through its central switch — works by dividing access into equal slots of time. Stations with messages to send are assigned time slots, during which they transmit a small portion, perhaps no more than a single bit, of their message. The simplified examples at right show two sequential time slots from the combined A-to-D and C-to-B transmissions illustrated above. During A's time slot *(top)*, the central switch opens logic gates *(blue)* to clear a route for input from A's line and output to D's. Station A releases the specified amount of data, and the data flows through the switch *(red arrow)*. In the next time slot *(bottom)*, the A and D gates are closed, and a path is established from C to B *(purple arrow)*. Alternating in rapid succession, the time slots will continue sending chunks of data until the two messages are complete.

islands. "What I did," Metcalfe explained later, "was take the basic Alohanet concept and add a few wrinkles and in particular apply it to the problem of connecting computers within a building rather than throughout the Hawaiian Islands." Metcalfe drew the name Ethernet from the long-ago-discredited idea that, as he put it, "there must be a universally present passive medium called ether, even in the emptiness of space, through which electromagnetic waves propagate."

In his Ethernet concept, each station — consisting of a computer or peripheral device such as a printer — connects through a short cable to a transceiver, a device capable of both transmitting and receiving data packets. Each of the network's transceivers taps into a long cable that links them all together. Unlike packet switching as practiced by the VAN — in which intermediate nodes on the network route data packets to a particular destination — an Ethernet computer "broadcasts" its packets to all stations tied into the cable. Each station snares only the packets addressed to it, ignoring the others (pages 58-59).

Hoping to make Ethernet an industry-wide standard for LANs, Xerox for a nominal fee licensed other companies to create networks based on the system. One of the licensees was Metcalfe, who had left Xerox to start 3Com Corporation — for Computer Communication Compatibility — which manufactured software and hardware for Ethernet and other local area networks. In 1983, the Institute of Electrical and Electronic Engineers (IEEE) pronounced Ethernet, with some modifications, the first standard protocol for LANs — and helped make Metcalfe a multimillionaire.

Another IEEE-approved protocol defines a different kind of LAN technology. Known as the token-ring concept, it was sponsored by IBM in anticipation of marketing such a local area network in 1985. In contrast to the broadcast method of Ethernet, messages in the token-ring protocol are passed like a baton from station to station along a cable with the ends joined. The token is a special message that circulates around the ring when all stations are idle. Its arrival at a station indicates that the network is ready to accept data and gives the station permission to transmit. This system guarantees each station access to the network in rapid rotation (page 60).

THE BENEFITS OF STANDARDIZATION

The cost of local area networks has remained high. Part of the expense lies in the installation and maintenance of such systems, costs that are difficult to reduce. The prices of hardware and software for LANs have also been a factor but might well become less of an issue if one or two protocols — Ethernet and the token-ring network, for example — were to become widespread. Settling on a couple of methods of networking would encourage semiconductor manufacturers to integrate, into a handful of inexpensive computer chips, the complex circuitry necessary to connect computers. And the cost of equipment such as printers and storage devices would decrease, inasmuch as manufacturers of these peripherals could make each product in only two versions rather than many and still appeal to all LAN users.

Nonetheless, the LAN market has remained fragmented. In spite of the recommendations from a trade or professional organization such as the IEEE, suppliers vie for the local-networking dollar by producing proprietary products;

62

in the absence of expensive customizing by means of special software, these products tend to be compatible with only a limited range of machines.

Almost inevitably, each supplier promotes its own protocol in an attempt to establish it as a de facto standard. More often than not, the tactic succeeds only in postponing the emergence of a universal protocol. Occasionally, however, a product will be so popular that, in effect, it writes the specifications for the competition. After the D. C. Hayes Company in Norcross, Georgia, marketed the first desktop-computer intelligent modem (one capable of automatic dialing and answering), independent programmers wrote communications software compatible with its set of protocols; other modem manufacturers then had to make their machines similar to the Hayes device so that they would work with the new Hayes-inspired software. In a short time, the Hayes-modem protocol became a national standard in the United States.

Even a user of computers sometimes possesses the influence, will or economic clout to force a standard upon the market. One unsurprising example is the federal government. Another is the computer industry's biggest commercial customer, General Motors, which spends hundreds of millions of dollars each year on computer automation. Thanks to GM's buying power and bold initiative during the 1980s, it now seems all but certain that a single set of protocols will prevail for linking computers, robots and other smart machines into integrated networks for manufacturing. According to David Clark, a senior research scientist at M.I.T., "This is the first time a consumer has tried to impose standardization on the computer world."

CHOREOGRAPHED FACTORIES

Known as MAP — for Manufacturing Automation Protocol — the GM system is a specialized version of a local area network that the company has made available to anyone who wishes to use it. However, this LAN is designed not to link office equipment but to choreograph the intricate mechanical dance on the factory floor. It coordinates the work of computer-controlled machine tools, plans the rounds of automated carts that carry parts from warehouse to assembly line, dictates the motions of robots that weld or paint automobile bodies, and governs the activities of computers that control inventory and monitor the entire manufacturing process.

GM set up a task force to develop MAP in 1980 because engineers and executives saw that their vision of a manufacturing process, controlled from beginning to end by computers, was foundering. Each auto plant was becoming an archipelago of automation islands — clusters of machines that operated independently rather than in concert. More often than not, the gaps between these isolated networks had to be bridged by the "sneaker network" — fleet-footed humans carrying programs and data from one machine to another. A unified production system combining the new technologies of computer-aided design, engineering and manufacturing, lay somewhere beyond the horizon.

In 1982, General Motors announced its intention to establish MAP networks in all its plants and asked equipment suppliers to adhere to its protocols for interconnections. In essence, MAP is a variation of IBM's token-ring technology that does not require the ends of the cable connecting stations on the network to be joined. Instead, the machines plug into a long, open-ended cable called a bus by way of black boxes and printed circuit boards that incorporate elaborate software and convert each machine's signals into a language understandable to all. The token-passing technique regulates traffic on the network and prevents time-consuming message collisions.

When several computer manufacturers with a proprietary interest in preserving their own network protocols balked at implementing GM's, the auto maker flexed its economic muscle. In effect, the company informed the recalcitrants that they would adhere to MAP or cease being General Motors suppliers. The company also rallied scores of other influential firms, such as Chrysler, Boeing and Eastman Kodak, to the MAP standard. In the end, the resistance vanished, and more than 100 computer hardware manufacturers endorsed MAP.

MAP-PING THE ASSEMBLY LINE
GM began installing limited versions of MAP networks at some of its plants in 1984. Two years later, the first full-scale networks went on-line at the company's axle-manufacturing plant in Saginaw, Michigan, and the truck and bus assembly lines in Pontiac. With MAP in place, the plant's managers could accomplish in minutes the tooling changes necessary for the machines to produce a different kind of axle—a massive switchover that formerly took three days.

Looking beyond 1990, when GM is scheduled to have placed MAP in control of all its manufacturing facilities, some communications specialists expect the company to set a far more ambitious goal: computerized division of labor on a global scale. An automobile might be designed by the Italians, acquire its engine from the Japanese and be assembled in the U.S. The entire process, from blueprints to delivery of the finished product, would be orchestrated by computers and other smart machines connected in a worldwide MAP network based not only on long-distance telephone lines but on satellite communications and on the most versatile communications medium yet devised—glass filaments that carry computer data as pulses of light.

Packet Switching: An Efficient Way to Shuttle Data

Human telephone conversations are characterized by irregular pauses, alternating with irregular bursts of speech; overall, however, the transmission of voice signals is relatively constant. The traditional method of creating and maintaining a telephone connection has been circuit switching, a technique in which a transmission line is opened between two parties and held open until their communication is finished. Even during moments of silence, when the line between the two parties is temporarily idle, the circuit remains dedicated to their exclusive use. Although transmission time is essentially wasted during those idle moments, the loss is insignificant in relation to the overall rate of information flow.

Many computer communications, in contrast, are characterized by relatively long pauses between short bursts of transmission. During a credit check, for example, a department store's terminal might transmit a customer's identification number to a central data bank, then wait several seconds to receive a quick spurt of credit information. Excluding other electronic traffic from the transmission line while the data bank processes the store's inquiry — as would be the case if a circuit-switched connection were used — is costly and inefficient. A technique known as packet switching prevents such wastefulness by allowing multiple computer communications to travel over the same link in a specially organized network.

Packet switching derives its name from the way a message is split into many segments, or packets, each of which is handled as a separate communication. Not only may packets from many different messages be interleaved on a common transmission line, but packets from the same message may travel along several different lines. As illustrated on the following pages, network designers employ a number of different programming strategies to route transmissions through the system and to ensure that each segmented message arrives intact at its destination.

Designed for Economy and Flexibility

As the number of machines increases, point-to-point connection becomes less practical. In the system at right, each of the six machines requires ports, or plug-in slots, for five transmission lines; 15 lines are needed to link the machines to one another.

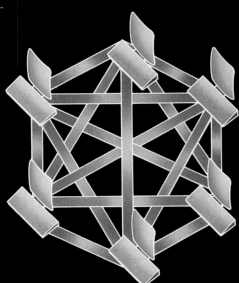

Point-to-point connections are adequate when the number of communicating elements are few. The direct link shown near right between two computers (represented by terminals) might also be used to connect a computer with a printer or other peripheral device.

A network that uses relay stations, or nodes, eliminates the dense tangle of direct connections. The scheme shown below and on the following pages represents a communication system dispersed over a wide geographical area.

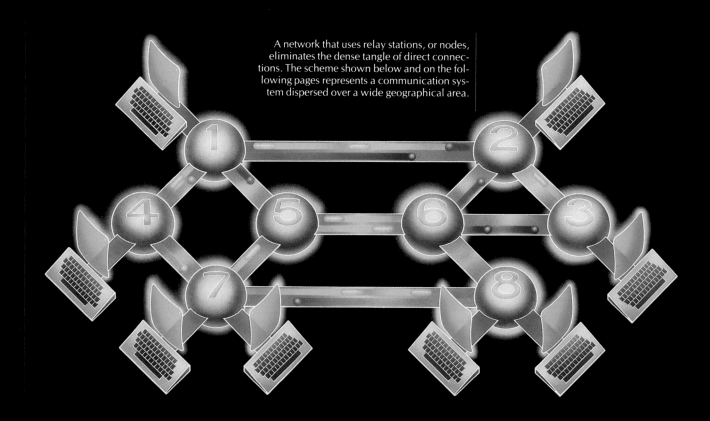

Computer networks were developed to allow users in several locations to share computing facilities and resources, whether the users are on different floors of the same building or in cities thousands of miles apart. The alternative to a network is a point-to-point system, in which each computer is directly linked to every other computer, terminal or peripheral with which it must communicate. Such a configuration quickly grows unwieldy: The number of direct links required can be found by the formula $N(N - 1)/2$, where N is the number of communicating machines in the system. For example, enabling 10 computers to communicate with one another in a point-to-point system would require 45 separate lines; a network linking the machines to a central relay, or node, could provide the same service with only 10 connections.

In a packet-switching network, electronic messages are divided into small segments called data packets, typically containing a few thousand bits of data apiece. Depending on the system involved, the packets in a given message may all follow a single route, or they may take a variety of transmission paths to the destination. In any case, each packet travels independently as the system attempts to move the entire message through the network with maximum efficiency.

The Cast of Essential Characters

A packet-switching communication network is made up of stations, nodes and transmission paths. Stations, represented here and on the following pages as simple terminals, may also include computers and peripherals such as printers. Nodes are usually special processors that act as the network's traffic directors, receiving packets from stations or from other nodes and routing them to their destinations. Packets come in several forms: data packets, which hold parts of messages, and various control packets, some of which initiate and maintain communication. Transmission paths are the lines along which packets travel.

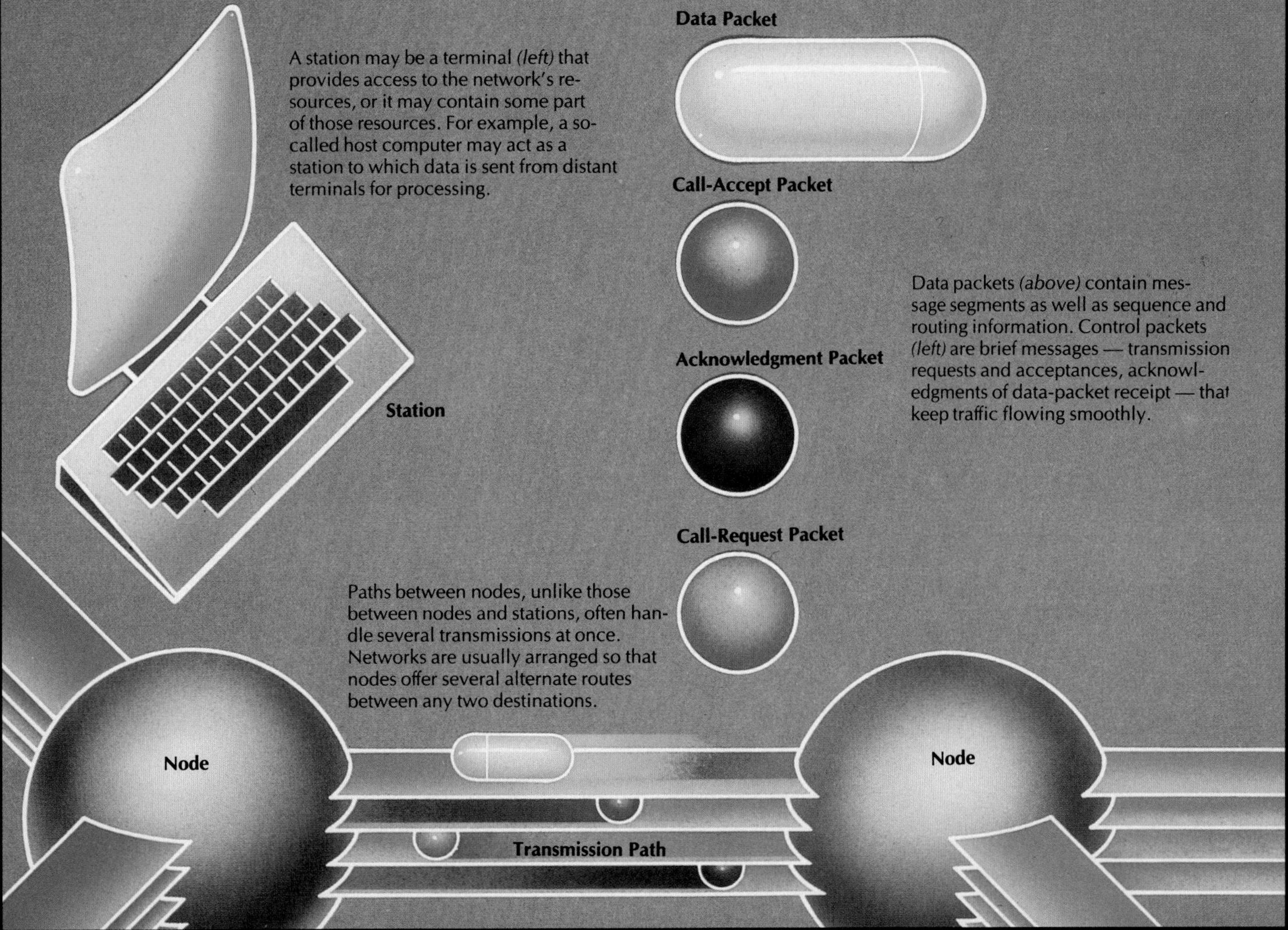

A station may be a terminal *(left)* that provides access to the network's resources, or it may contain some part of those resources. For example, a so-called host computer may act as a station to which data is sent from distant terminals for processing.

Data packets *(above)* contain message segments as well as sequence and routing information. Control packets *(left)* are brief messages — transmission requests and acceptances, acknowledgments of data-packet receipt — thai keep traffic flowing smoothly.

Paths between nodes, unlike those between nodes and stations, often handle several transmissions at once. Networks are usually arranged so that nodes offer several alternate routes between any two destinations.

The Critical Job
of a Network Node

Nodes in a data-communication network are comparable to the mechanical switches that shift railway trains from track to track. To find the destination of each data packet as it arrives, the node reads the control data located in a portion of the packet called the header. The node sends the packet out on the appropriate transmission path based on a calculation of the optimum route to that destination. The calculation may be carried out by each individual node or by a supervisory node that instructs subordinate nodes accordingly. In some systems, optimum routes between all stations in the network are predetermined and fixed; in networks that use so-called adaptive routing *(pages 74-75)*, transmission paths are subject to change depending on traffic conditions.

Because they act as both senders and receivers, nodes are designed to perform several tasks to ensure the integrity of communications. For example, upon receiving a data packet, a node must inspect it for any electrical damage or distortion that may have occurred during transmission; if the packet has not arrived intact, the node requests the sending node or station to retransmit it. Conversely, before sending a packet on, the node makes and stores a copy of it in case retransmission is necessary. To handle network traffic systematically, nodes hold data packets in temporary storage areas called buffers. Incoming packets queue up in a buffer while the node reads their headers and checks for damage; outgoing packets queue in a buffer with packets departing along the same path.

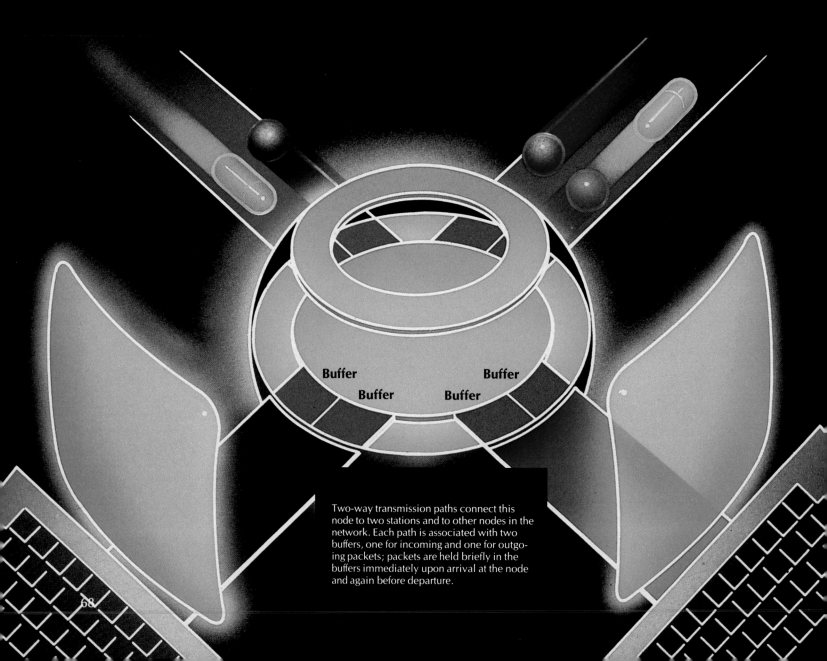

Buffer   **Buffer**

Buffer   **Buffer**

Two-way transmission paths connect this node to two stations and to other nodes in the network. Each path is associated with two buffers, one for incoming and one for outgoing packets; packets are held briefly in the buffers immediately upon arrival at the node and again before departure.

The node inspects an arriving packet's header to determine its destination; when the packet is ready to be sent on, the node will move it to the correct outbound queue.

To find errors, the node can perform a calculation on the packet's bits. If the result, or checksum, matches the sum in the packet's header, the transmission was error-free.

The node then sends an acknowledgment packet to the sending node or station, to let it know that the data packet arrived intact.

To select the next leg of the packet's journey, the node can perform its own route calculations, receive instructions from a supervisory node or look up the route in a table.

Before transmitting the packet, the node makes a copy of it; if the packet is damaged en route, the node can send the backup.

When an acknowledgment packet indicates that the data packet has been safely received, the node can erase the backup by overwriting, or reusing, the memory space holding the copy.

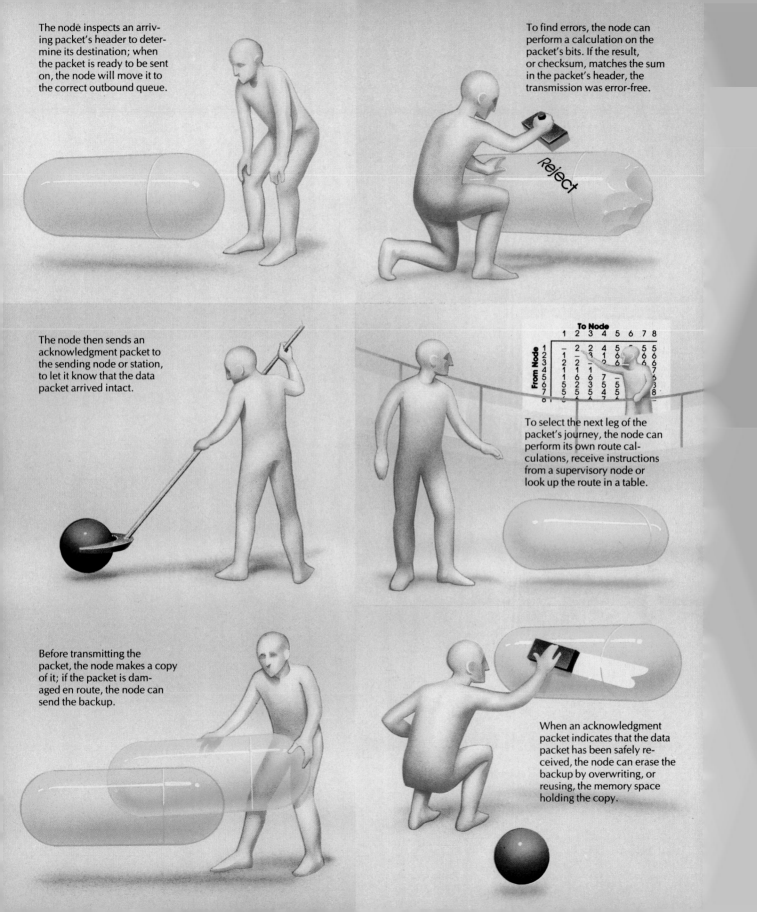

ending Messages on Virtual Circuit

A virtual circuit is so named because packet-switching trans mission via this method resembles the continuous connection of the traditional circuit-switched telephone system. (An alter native packet-switching method known as the datagram i described on pages 72-73.) To initiate a virtual-circuit trans mission, a station sends a call-request packet — a contro packet announcing the station's desire to send a message — to the nearest node. In the example below, Station A sends a call-request packet *(purple)* to Node 1 asking to communicate with Station B. Node 1 has a choice of three paths along which it can transmit the request: to Nodes 2, 4 or 5. Using whatever routing-decision method is employed by the net

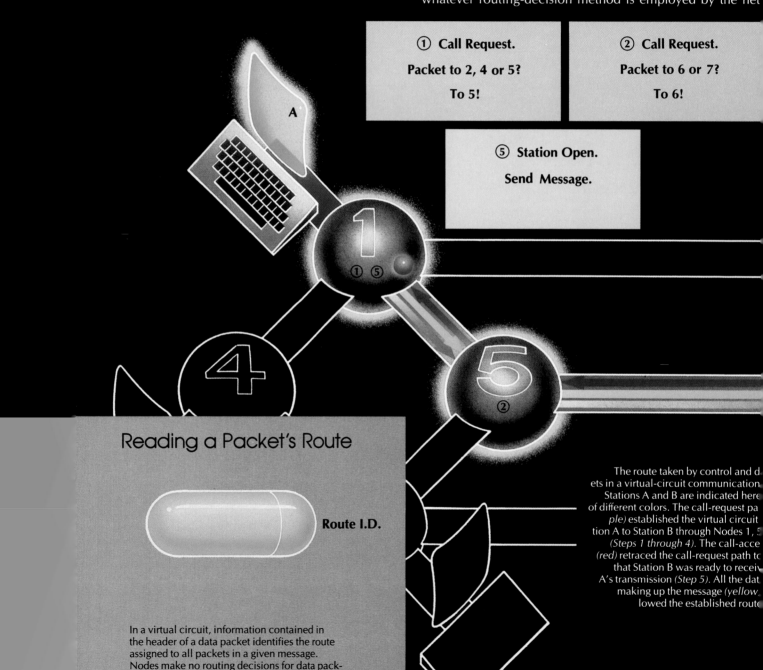

① **Call Request.**

Packet to 2, 4 or 5?

To 5!

② **Call Request.**

Packet to 6 or 7?

To 6!

⑤ **Station Open.**

Send Message.

Reading a Packet's Route

Route I.D.

In a virtual circuit, information contained in the header of a data packet identifies the route assigned to all packets in a given message. Nodes make no routing decisions for data packets; each simply reads the header and sends the packet on to the next designated node.

The route taken by control and da ets in a virtual-circuit communication. Stations A and B are indicated here of different colors. The call-request pa *ple)* established the virtual circuit tion A to Station B through Nodes 1, 5 *(Steps 1 through 4)*. The call-acce *(red)* retraced the call-request path to that Station B was ready to recei A's transmission *(Step 5)*. All the dat making up the message *(yellow* lowed the established route work, Node 1 elects to forward the control packet to Node 5. Following similar procedures, Node 5 forwards the call request to Node 6, which in turn sends it to Node 8, the nearest node to Station B.

Finding that Station B is open to communication, Node 8 sends a call-accept packet *(red)* back along the path established by the call-request packet, from Node 8 to Nodes 6, 5 and 1; the nodes do not have to make any new routing decisions. All the packets in the message from Station A to Station B will now follow the trail blazed by the call-request packet. At each node, data packets will be checked for errors, acknowledgments will go out to verify receipt of each undamaged packet, and the packets will be copied before being sent on.

Unlike a true circuit-switched transmission — which commits the line to one sender and one receiver — a virtual circuit can accommodate many communications by interleaving packets from different messages. In addition, a given node can be involved in several virtual circuits simultaneously. Thus all data packets must carry information in their headers identifying the paths they are to follow. When the last packet of a message arrives at its destination, the station sends a control packet back on the route to break the virtual circuit used for that communication.

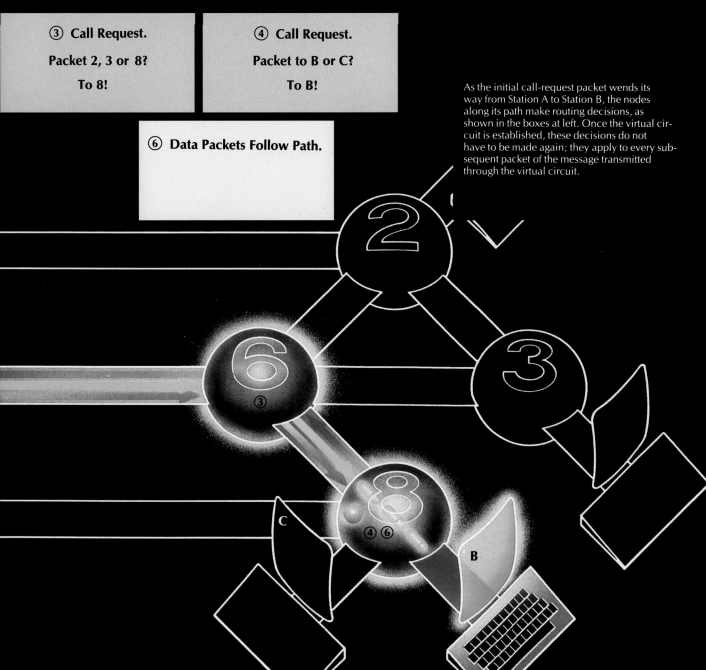

③ **Call Request.**

Packet 2, 3 or 8?

To 8!

④ **Call Request.**

Packet to B or C?

To B!

⑥ **Data Packets Follow Path.**

As the initial call-request packet wends its way from Station A to Station B, the nodes along its path make routing decisions, as shown in the boxes at left. Once the virtual circuit is established, these decisions do not have to be made again; they apply to every subsequent packet of the message transmitted through the virtual circuit.

The Advantages of Datagram Transmission

A virtual circuit is preferred for a long and essentially one-way session, as when a large quantity of information is being keyed into a central data bank from a remote terminal. With many transactions, however, such as the short, back-and-forth communications of a credit check, the datagram method is more efficient, for several reasons.

First, datagram transmission does not require an exchange of call-request and call-accept packets to establish a path between the sending and receiving stations. In terms of system overhead, such control packets become more costly the shorter the message.

In a datagram network that employs adaptive routing

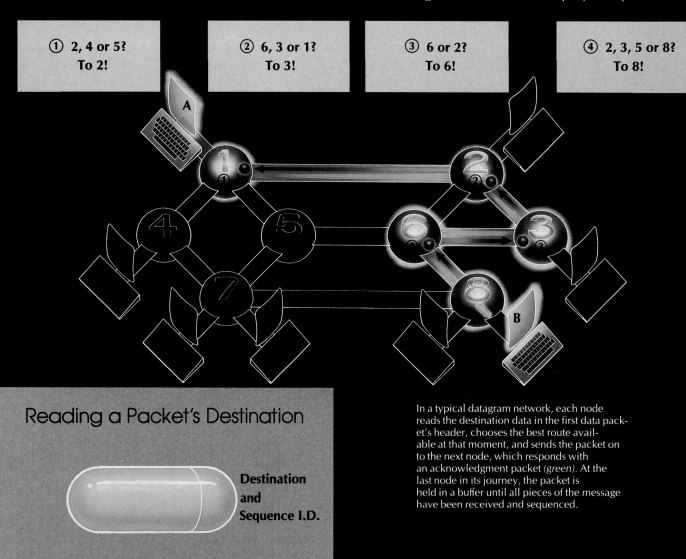

① 2, 4 or 5?
To 2!

② 6, 3 or 1?
To 3!

③ 6 or 2?
To 6!

④ 2, 3, 5 or 8?
To 8!

Reading a Packet's Destination

Destination and Sequence I.D.

The header of a typical datagram packet contains coded numbers representing the packet's ultimate destination and its place in the message sequence. Unlike the header of a virtual-circuit data packet, it does not contain routing information; each node will make routing decisions as the packet moves through the network.

In a typical datagram network, each node reads the destination data in the first data packet's header, chooses the best route available at that moment, and sends the packet on to the next node, which responds with an acknowledgment packet (green). At the last node in its journey, the packet is held in a buffer until all pieces of the message have been received and sequenced.

(pages 74-75), another benefit accrues. Since no single path holds for the duration of a session, the header of each data packet does not carry information spelling out each step of the packet's route. Instead, it simply carries a sequence number and the address of the packet's destination; the network routes each packet separately, making a new routing decision each time a packet arrives at a node. Depending on the network's configuration, 10 consecutive packets in a datagram message could travel to their common destination along 10 different paths, being resequenced if necessary at the end. By monitoring conditions on the network and revising routing decisions based on updated information, the datagram meth-od not only can avoid congested areas, but also is less vulnerable to system malfunctions; if part of the network breaks down, datagram packets can simply be rerouted.

In another form of datagram packet switching, routes may be fixed (pages 76-77), with the possibility that the system can choose between two fixed alternatives. This method is less flexible than full-fledged adaptive routing but has the advantage of cutting down on the computation required to update and revise routes.

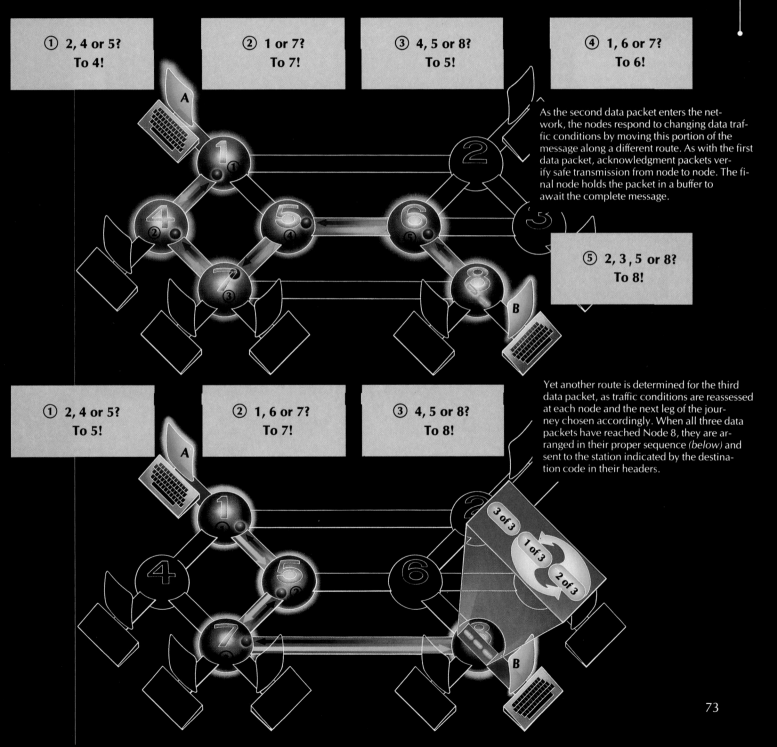

As the second data packet enters the network, the nodes respond to changing data traffic conditions by moving this portion of the message along a different route. As with the first data packet, acknowledgment packets verify safe transmission from node to node. The final node holds the packet in a buffer to await the complete message.

Yet another route is determined for the third data packet, as traffic conditions are reassessed at each node and the next leg of the journey chosen accordingly. When all three data packets have reached Node 8, they are arranged in their proper sequence (below) and sent to the station indicated by the destination code in their headers.

73

The Responsiveness of Adaptive Routing

The datagram network illustrated on the preceding pages used adaptive routing, a technique that allows a network to respond to changing traffic conditions. If packets are backed up in a buffer at a given node, the system can send traffic through other nodes until the bottleneck clears. Similar re-routing can occur if a transmission path is malfunctioning.

The particular variety of adaptive routing illustrated here employs a set of programming instructions called a forward-search algorithm. In this scheme, the network keeps track of the cost (measured in delay time) of various routes from and to different nodes. As packets make their way along the network, the forward-search algorithm is periodically used to calculate

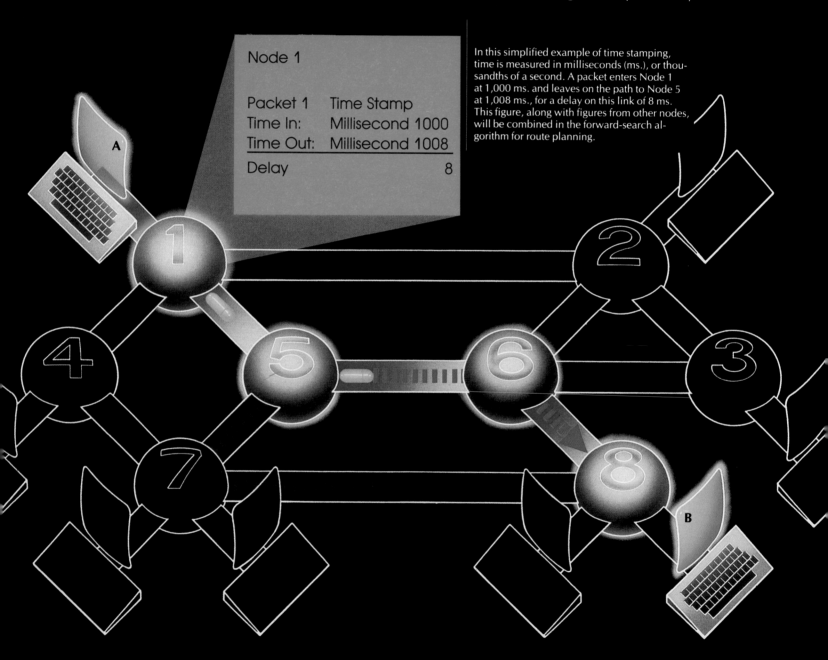

Node 1

Packet 1	Time Stamp
Time In:	Millisecond 1000
Time Out:	Millisecond 1008
Delay	8

In this simplified example of time stamping, time is measured in milliseconds (ms.), or thousandths of a second. A packet enters Node 1 at 1,000 ms. and leaves on the path to Node 5 at 1,008 ms., for a delay on this link of 8 ms. This figure, along with figures from other nodes, will be combined in the forward-search algorithm for route planning.

the lowest-cost route from a given node to a given packet's destination. Adaptive routing of this kind may be overseen by a supervisory node that collects delay-time data from throughout the network. Alternatively, the responsibility for monitoring delays and calculating routes may be distributed among the nodes in the network, as shown here.

One method of measuring delay time is called time stamping. Each node monitors the time a packet arrives in the node's incoming buffer and the time it departs from the outgoing buffer, and then reports the amount of delay either to a supervisory node or, in a distributed system, to other nodes in the network. In either case, the information is plugged into the forward-search algorithm. (Although delay time at nodes is the only factor shown in the simplified calculations below, in practice, the forward-search algorithm would also take into account other factors, such as transmission time between nodes.) By compiling and periodically updating delay data from every node, the network is able to calculate at any moment the quickest route between any two points.

Moment 1, From Node 1

To Node	Path	Link Delay	Total Delay Cost
2	1-2	8	8
	1-5-6-2	8 + 5 + 6	19
	1-5-7-8-6-2	8 + 4 + 4 + 4 + 6	26
5	1-5	8	8
	1-2-6-5	8 + 6 + 5	19
	1-2-6-8-7-5	8 + 6 + 4 + 4 + 4	26
6	1-2-6	8 + 6	14
	1-5-6	8 + 5	13
	1-5-7-8-6	8 + 4 + 4 + 4	20
7	1-5-7	8 + 4	12
	1-5-6-8-7	8 + 5 + 4 + 4	21
	1-2-6-5-7	8 + 6 + 5 + 4	23
	1-2-6-8-7	8 + 6 + 4 + 4	22
8	1-2-6-8	8 + 6 + 4	18
	1-2-6-5-7-8	8 + 6 + 5 + 4 + 4	27
	1-5-6-8	8 + 5 + 4	17
	1-5-7-8	**8 + 4 + 4**	**16**

Shown here are the delays (in milliseconds) along some of the possible paths from Node 1 to Node 8 of the network illustrated on the opposite page. (Large networks typically do not calculate delays along all possible paths; the computational effort required could in itself cause greater delays.) At this particular moment, the least-cost path of those considered for sending a message from Node 1 to Node 8 is via Nodes 5 and 7 (depicted on the network by a broken blue line).

The chart at right, representing a later instant, reveals changes in the delays along paths from Node 5 to Nodes 1, 2, 6, 7 and 8. Compared with the chart above, the delay time from Node 5 to Node 7 has increased by 6 ms., from 4 ms. to 10 ms. Given this information, the forward-search algorithm recalculates the least-cost path and finds that it is now quicker to send a packet from Node 5 to Node 8 via Node 6 (broken orange line), rather than via Node 7.

Moment 2, From Node 5

To Node	Path	Link Delay	Total Delay Cost
1	5-1	8	8
	5-6-2-1	5 + 6 + 8	19
	5-7-8-6-2-1	10 + 4 + 4 + 6 + 8	32
2	5-6-2	5 + 6	11
	5-1-2	8 + 8	16
	5-7-8-6-2	10 + 4 + 4 + 6	24
6	5-6	5	5
	5-7-8-6	10 + 4 + 4	18
	5-1-2-6	8 + 8 + 6	22
7	5-7	10	10
	5-1-2-6-8-7	8 + 8 + 6 + 4 + 4	30
	5-6-8-7	5 + 4 + 4	13
8	**5-6-8**	**5 + 4**	**9**
	5-1-2-6-8	8 + 8 + 6 + 4	26
	5-7-8	10 + 4	14

The Simplicity of Static Routing

An alternative to adaptive routing is static routing, a technique that is more vulnerable to malfunctions and congestion, but reduces a network's overhead by relieving the nodes of many computational responsibilities. Two types of static routing — fixed routing and flooding — are illustrated below.

With fixed routing, the network programmer establishes a directory of optimum routes to and from every point in the network. Each node simply reads a packet's header to learn its destination, then either looks up that destination in a stored directory or receives instructions from a supervisory node, as shown below. Thus, every message and every packet of a message sent from Station A to Station B will follow the same

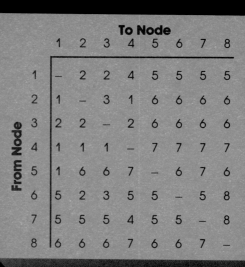

	To Node							
From Node	1	2	3	4	5	6	7	8
1	–	2	2	4	5	5	5	5
2	1	–	3	1	6	6	6	6
3	2	2	–	2	6	6	6	6
4	1	1	1	–	7	7	7	7
5	1	6	6	7	–	6	7	6
6	5	2	3	5	5	–	5	8
7	5	5	5	4	5	5	–	8
8	6	6	6	7	6	6	7	–

In this fixed-routing directory — stored at Node 2, the supervisory node in this example — sending nodes are listed in the leftmost column, receiving nodes in the top row. (In a distributed scheme, each node would store only the row that listed the optimum next stage for transmission to another node.) If Node 1 receives a packet destined for Node 8, the supervisory node consults the directory and instructs Node 1 to send the packet to Node 5. Node 5, in turn, is told to send the packet to Node 6, and so on; the supervisory node checks the directory for the route one node at a time.

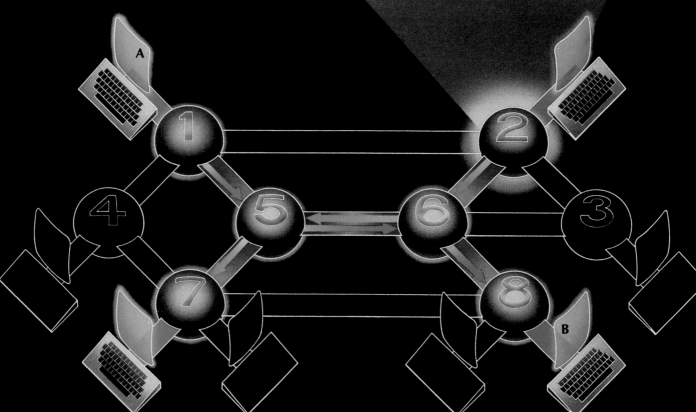

route. (In networks that employ a variation of fixed routing, there may be two or more routes — with predetermined priority — to choose from.)

Flooding is useful in cases where one message must go to all stations or in an emergency when, for example, part of a military network might be damaged. Each node makes several copies of all message packets it receives, and sends one along every transmission path except the path a packet came in on. An obvious drawback to flooding is that the network can become clogged as the number of copies increases. One method for dealing with this problem is to program the destination node to accept only one copy of each packet, and to destroy duplicates as they arrive. (Each original packet and each copy has a unique identifier.) Another solution to the clogging problem is to tag packets with a so-called hop-count number equal to some large value, such as the number of nodes in the network; each node reduces by one the hop count of every incoming packet and destroys any packet whose hop count reaches zero.

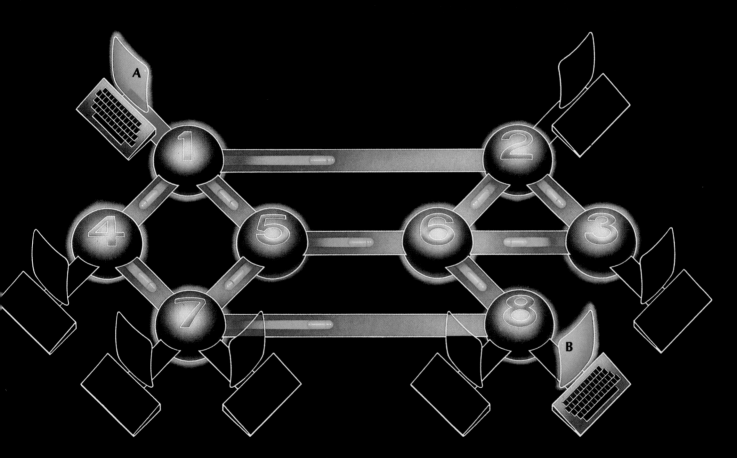

In a flooding scheme, each node obeys a sequence of instructions that might run as follows for each packet it receives: 1. Inspect the address in the packet's header. 2. If this node is the packet's destination, forward it to the appropriate station. 3. If this is not the destination, deduct 1 from the hop count. 4. If the resulting value is greater than 0, make copies and send them along all routes except the one the packet arrived on. 5. If the new value is 0, destroy the packet.

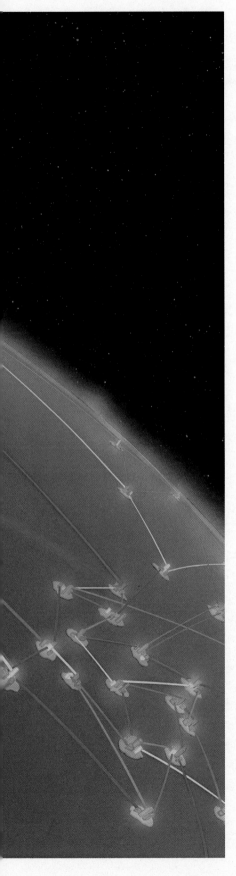

Fibers and Waves to Span the Globe

In the predawn hours of July 10, 1962, a Delta rocket lifted a 175-pound satellite about the size of a beach ball from Cape Canaveral, Florida, into an orbit several thousand miles above the earth. There was nothing extraordinary about launching a satellite; the United States and the Soviet Union had been doing so since 1957. But this one was something special. Named *Telstar,* it was the first satellite capable of receiving and transmitting voice, television and data signals across the span of the Atlantic Ocean.

Built and operated entirely by Bell Laboratories, *Telstar* had thousands of electronic components packed inside, enabling the satellite to perform a variety of tasks. Some of the components generated a radio signal, a beacon that allowed the satellite to be tracked by antennas on earth. Other components monitored the satellite's operation, sending readings to earth piggyback on the beacon signal. But the bulk of *Telstar's* electronics was dedicated to communications. When *Telstar* received a signal beamed from earth, a device called a transponder aboard the satellite amplified the message more than 10 billion times and immediately rebroadcast it toward earth.

Several large antennas called earth stations, situated in the United States, Britain and France, handled communications with *Telstar.* The nerve center of the earth-station network was an installation built by Bell Labs near Andover, Maine. Information about the satellite's progress around the earth raced to Andover over telephone lines from tracking stations around the world. There, a computer digested the data and instantly calculated where on the horizon the satellite would appear. The computer then aimed at that spot an antenna shaped something like a giant ear trumpet or horn. As soon as tracking antennas at Andover picked up *Telstar's* beacon, signaling that the satellite had risen above the horizon, transmission through the horn antenna could begin.

The earth station at Andover was working perfectly the morning *Telstar* blasted into orbit. But before Bell technicians could put the equipment to use, they had to endure a nerve-racking delay. Because of *Telstar's* launch trajectory, the satellite was not scheduled to come into view until its sixth orbit, more than 16 hours after the launch. "It was a long day for the Bell system crew at Andover, making last-minute adjustments, exercising their equipment, and watching the preparations to broadcast their success or failure to the world," a Bell history of the event later recounted.

In Washington, D.C., a large body of dignitaries waited expectantly for the first transmissions from *Telstar.* For the demonstration, signals were to be sent from Andover to *Telstar* and back again. They would then travel by way of terrestrial long-distance telephone connections to the auditorium of the Daughters of the

American Revolution building in Washington, where Bell officials, politicians and other guests had gathered. AT&T chairman Frederick Kappel, who was observing events from Andover, had also invited the media to cover *Telstar's* first transmissions. Playing to the public had worried some of the company's engineers. "It was considered very hazardous," one of them recalled, "because many space projects don't work out the first time. But the Bell Labs people had a lot of confidence in *Telstar.*"

At 9:18 on the evening of the launch, the Andover earth station detected *Telstar's* beacon and locked the giant horn antenna onto the target. At 9:30, Kappel placed a long-distance telephone call from Andover through *Telstar* to Vice President Lyndon Johnson in Washington. "How do you hear me?" Kappel asked. "You're coming through nicely," the vice president replied.

Then, at 9:33, the most technologically demanding moment of the evening got under way. At the DAR auditorium, all eyes were fixed on a television screen as a picture of an American flag waving outside Andover was sent over conventional telephone circuits to Washington. That signal faded and was replaced by a view of the flag sent by way of *Telstar.* There was no doubt about it. The signal transmitted more than 44,000 miles through space was as clear as the one sent a few hundred miles by land.

TELECOMMUNICATIONS MILESTONES

In the next four months, *Telstar* achieved a long list of firsts in the telecommunications field. It relayed television signals between the United States and Europe, showing an estimated 200 million European viewers such images as a baseball game in Chicago, the world's fair in Seattle and the Statue of Liberty. It conducted the world's first transatlantic telephone conversation by satellite. It even probed the radiation belts around the earth to learn more about the operating environment for future communications satellites.

Almost lost among these milestones was a series of tests that pointed toward an important future use of satellites — the transmission of computer data. During one 19-minute transmission from France to the United States, *Telstar* relayed almost a billion bits of data, the equivalent of about one and a half million words per minute, with only one error. The information, which included data such as medical records, bookkeeping files and instructions for programming machine tools, was sent from the memory of a French computer to a U.S. computer's memory and to a magnetic-tape storage device connected to it.

The birth of the communications satellite was a banner event in the history of modern telecommunications. But satellites are only one of several transmission techniques that have remade communications since World War II. Before the 1950s, virtually all electronic messages traveled over wires. Today the majority of long-distance telephone calls travel through the air as microwaves. International communications satellites provide more than half of the telephone and television links between the United States and overseas countries, and domestic satellites offer a wide variety of services for American business. Since the early 1980s, pulses of light traveling through optical fibers of glass clearer than crystal have carried an ever-increasing share of long-distance communications. So advantageous are these methods of moving information from one place to another that traditional copper wires may someday become obsolete.

The new transmission media evolved mainly to handle the bread and butter of telecommunications: voice and video signals. But as computer communications burgeoned in the 1950s and 1960s, microwaves, satellites and optical fibers became a focus of attention for people who had to send great quantities of data quickly. Businesses purchased microwave links from companies specializing in data transmissions. Digital satellite networks were established to connect computers in widely separated locations. Optical fibers began to link computers and peripheral equipment in local area networks. The result has been a steady expansion in the capabilities of computers — an expansion that shows every sign of continuing.

THE MICROWAVE CONNECTION

The earliest of the new transmission media can trace its roots to the same event that gave rise to the first general-purpose electronic computer: World War II. In the years before the war, British scientists developed a way to ascertain the location of aircraft by beaming radio waves into the sky. An extremely accurate clock measured the time it took the signal to reach an aircraft and be reflected to the transmitting antenna; from the elapsed time, the distance of the plane could be calculated. Known in Britain as radiolocation, this technique eventually acquired the name given it by American scientists working on such systems — radio detection and ranging, or radar.

By the beginning of the war, unbeknownst to the Germans, a sophisticated radar network kept a constant vigil on the entire east coast of Britain. During the Battle of Britain in August and September of 1940, about 600 British aircraft were able to stymie 3,000 aircraft of the Luftwaffe, largely because the British, using the information provided by their radar system, could dispatch exactly as many planes as were needed to exactly the right spot. Frustrated and mystified by the continual successes of the British fighter pilots, the Luftwaffe eventually postponed plans to invade Britain and switched to night bombing. Thus the development of radar played a key role in keeping Britain from being overrun early in the conflict, drastically altering the course of the war.

Throughout the war, British and American scientists pursued the development of radar systems that used radio signals of higher and higher frequency. The shorter wavelengths of these high-frequency transmissions could pinpoint a plane more accurately than signals of longer wavelength. Moreover, high-frequency signals required smaller antennas, allowing radar equipment to be installed on planes and ships. By the end of the war, the British and the Americans had shortened the wavelengths used in radars into what is known as the microwave range — electromagnetic waves with frequencies between one billion and 300 billion hertz (or gigahertz).

These high frequencies, besides being ideal for pinpointing aerial intruders, also promised to advance the field of electronic communications. The amount of information that any portion of the electromagnetic spectrum can carry depends on the range of frequencies it spans — its bandwidth. Microwaves between one billion and two billion hertz, for example, can carry a thousand times as much information as broadcast radio waves having frequencies between one million and two million hertz (or megahertz). The development of microwaves therefore multiplied radio communications capabilities many times over.

By the late 1940s, American communications and electronics companies had gained substantial knowledge of microwaves. Some had done considerable research on radar during the war, and one of them, AT&T, had built a microwave communications system used by the armed forces in both the European and the Pacific theaters. So rich was the potential of this system that not long after peace had been reestablished, the company turned its attention to civilian microwave applications. But AT&T was not alone. Several companies were ready and able to jump into the microwave communications market.

Enthusiasm for the new medium was engendered not by the prospect of greatly expanded computer communications, since computers were then still in their infancy, but by a technology that was poised to engulf the nation: television. At the end of the war, there were only nine television stations in the United States. Within three years there were 36, with another 70 under construction. Like radio stations before them, television stations needed a way to transmit programs to one another for broadcast. But because transmitting a television signal requires about 1,000 times as much bandwidth as making a single telephone call, video communication needs exceeded the capacity of the wires and cables that made up the bulk of the postwar telephone network. The only wire circuits that could handle a television signal were made of coaxial cable. Invented by Bell Labs in the 1930s, this type of cable consists of two conductors—a solid one, which carries the signal, inside a hollow one, which shields the signal from interference. However, these cables were expensive to lay over extended distances and therefore were relatively scarce.

Then as now, connecting widely separated points by microwave differed greatly from linking them by wire or cable. Setting up a microwave circuit involves erecting a chain of towers, called repeaters, spaced 20 to 30 miles apart,

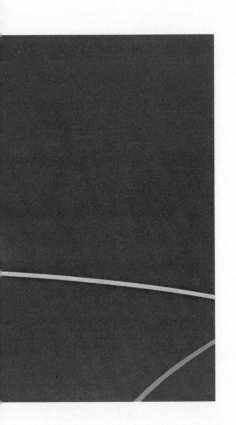

which is about as far as a microwave can travel before the horizon obstructs it. Each tower supports two or more smaller versions of the horn antenna used to send and receive signals from *Telstar*. These antennas gather in microwaves beamed from the preceding tower in the chain. A repeating device at the base of each tower amplifies the signals and sends them to another antenna on the tower, which beams them toward the next tower in the link. A long-distance telephone call crossing the United States by microwave makes more than 100 hops between such repeaters.

Although competitors beat AT&T to the punch, Ma Bell had acquired an abiding interest in microwaves. At that time, the company controlled virtually all of the long-distance lines in the United States. If other enterprises were allowed to set up microwave links, AT&T's monopoly would begin to crumble. For the telephone company, it was essential to find some way to reserve the establishment of microwave links for itself.

AT&T appealed to the Federal Communications Commission to limit the use of microwave frequencies to the common carriers, arguing that these frequencies were too few in number to allow all companies to use them. At first the FCC disagreed and freely issued experimental licenses for the new frequencies. But within a few years the regulators reversed themselves and adopted AT&T's position. Other companies, fearing that they could not compete profitably against AT&T under government regulation, dropped from the field. For the time being, AT&T had prevailed.

A CHINK IN THE ARMOR

Over the next decade or so, AT&T gradually made microwaves a mainstay of the telecommunications network in the United States. By 1956, more than 20 percent of Bell's capacity for handling long-distance telephone calls consisted of microwave channels. Intercity television was split 78 percent microwave and 22 percent coaxial cable. Computer data had also begun to travel over microwave channels, just as it does today when modems link widely separated computers through the telephone network.

More and more, as the use of microwaves grew, AT&T's near monopoly over them became a tempting target for others, largely because of a telephone-company practice known as rate averaging. In this method of setting prices, AT&T subsidized local service with part of the proceeds from its lucrative long-distance network. Also, the company charged uniform rates nationwide for long-distance services, even though the cost of providing them was much less per subscriber in densely populated regions than in rural areas. With the price to customers of long-distance service over busy routes substantially higher than the cost to AT&T, the possibility arose of luring away AT&T customers with lower rates. Especially ripe for the plucking were businesses that made extensive use of long-distance lines for data transmissions. Because computers sometimes communicated for hours at a stretch, telephone bills could become astronomical. Inflexible data-transmission speeds and frequent errors added to computer operators' woes. To one farsighted entrepreneur, disgruntlement over these problems offered the perfect opportunity to crack the market.

John Goeken was an unusual addition to the world of telecommunications, which after years of protected status had acquired a reputation for stodginess.

Outwardly raw and countrified, the former radio-equipment dealer from Joliet, Illinois, seemed an unlikely candidate to master the regulatory and legal thickets of telecommunications. But Goeken demonstrated a persistence that would confound his opponents.

In 1963, he and three electronics-salesmen friends founded Microwave Communications, Inc. (MCI) and petitioned the FCC for permission to build a microwave relay system between St. Louis and Chicago, one of AT&T's most heavily used routes. Goeken sought to draw several key distinctions between his new company and Ma Bell. He pointed out that MCI would offer a wider choice of bandwidths for computer communications. Also, though his system would be based on the same technology as AT&T's, it would not be saddled with antiquated equipment. Newer gear would produce fewer errors as data was transmitted. But Goeken did not try to disguise the fact that the new company would offer business users, its initial customers, voice and other transmission services in direct competition with AT&T. If Goeken had presented MCI as a regular business, the FCC would certainly have turned down his request. But Goeken's master stroke was to ask the FCC to recognize his fledgling company as a federally regulated common carrier.

AT&T, Western Union and the local telephone companies in St. Louis and Chicago fiercely contested MCI's request. They insisted that MCI was interested only in "skimming the cream" from the telecommunications market. If allowed to do so, they argued, companies like MCI would begin to offer reduced rates only along heavily traveled routes, cutting into the established carriers' profits and their wherewithal to subsidize less used communication links. Yet AT&T and the other common carriers would be forced by regulation to continue these marginal services.

Legal wrangling over the MCI request dragged on for six years. Finally, in 1969, the FCC commissioners, on a vote split four to three, granted Goeken permission to build the system he had proposed. FCC chairman Nicholas Johnson, who sided with Goeken, said that he wanted "to add a little salt and pepper of competition to the rather tasteless stew of regulatory protection that this commission and Bell have cooked up." Bell's last-minute appeals failed, and in 1971 Goeken began construction. William McGowan, a business consultant to the communications industry who began a long tenure as chairman of MCI's board of directors in 1968, later claimed that MCI had spent two million dollars building Goeken's dream — and five times that sum in legal and regulatory costs. But it was worth it. By 1973, MCI was an $80-million company, linking 40 cities from coast to coast.

A RELAY STATION IN SPACE
Besides having a greater capacity for data than most wires and cables, microwaves offered a second advantage to MCI and others that soon followed its example. There was no need to acquire a continuous right-of-way for cables. MCI could purchase or lease half an acre on a knoll every 20 to 30 miles between St. Louis and Chicago and build a relay tower there. However, what was advantageous for overland routes became a seemingly insurmountable obstacle at the seaside. For decades after the invention of microwave communications, there was no possibility of Europeans communicating with Americans by

microwave, for example, short of establishing a chain of 100 artificial islands across the Atlantic Ocean.

The first person to conceive of a solution to this problem was a young British researcher, engineer and wartime radar instructor, Arthur C. Clarke. In 1945, Clarke had not yet written any of the science fiction classics, including *2001: A Space Odyssey* and *Childhood's End,* that would later make him famous. But his experience with radar had taught him about microwaves, and he had seen the destruction visited upon London by German V-2 rockets near the end of the war. In an article written for the radio hobbyists' magazine *Wireless World,* Clarke merged these two developments into a single momentous idea. It would turn out to be one of the most prescient forecasts of future technology ever made.

Clarke envisioned rockets that could lift "space stations" into orbits circling the earth. There the stations could receive microwave signals from the ground and retransmit them toward receiving antennas. Boosted by rockets of varying power, the stations could occupy orbits having a wide range of altitudes. As Clarke pointed out, the time it takes a satellite to trace a circle in space with the earth as its center depends on how high the satellite is. For instance, a satellite at an altitude of 150 miles, a typical altitude for the space shuttle, takes approximately 90 minutes to return to the starting point of the circle. Earth's only natural satellite, the moon, orbits at a distance of 240,000 miles and takes about 28 days to make a single circuit.

MOTIONLESS IN THE SKY
Lying between these two orbits is one that intrigued Clarke. At an altitude of around 22,300 miles, a satellite completes a circle every 24 hours, the same time the earth requires to make a complete rotation. If the satellite is traveling in the same direction as the earth's rotation, it would seem to someone standing on the ground not to move at all. Such a satellite, Clarke wrote, would "remain fixed in the sky of a whole hemisphere and, unlike other heavenly bodies, would neither rise nor set." Because of this unusual attribute, this orbit has come to be known as a geostationary orbit. Among space scientists and engineers, it is also called the Clarke belt.

Geostationary orbits have a number of advantages for communications satellites, Clarke noted. For one, antennas on the earth could always point in the same direction to receive signals from the satellite, since it would appear to remain in the same place. (Actually, geostationary satellites wander slightly as they orbit; even so, tracking a satellite in the Clarke belt is far simpler than keeping tabs on satellites in other orbits.) Also, geostationary satellites are so far above the earth that they can "see" a great deal of it; according to Clarke's calculations, only three such satellites would be needed to cover virtually the entire globe.

However, Clarke also pointed out that several advances would have to be made before a communications satellite in geostationary orbit would be possible. First, there was the matter of launching such a vehicle. Lifting a satellite to an orbit so high would require rockets more powerful than any then available or on the drawing boards. Furthermore, a satellite would have to have a reliable and durable source of power in order to beam signals earthward. Nevertheless, Clarke was optimistic enough to believe that these obstacles could be overcome. "Many may consider the solution proposed in this discussion too farfetched to be taken seriously,'' he wrote. ''Such an attitude is unreasonable, as everything envisaged here is a logical extension of developments in the last ten years.''

For nearly a decade, Clarke's ideas hardly circulated outside the close-knit community of radio and space buffs. Then, in 1954, the same notions occurred independently to someone else—another engineer who had written science fiction in his off hours. In that year, John Pierce of Bell Labs was asked to address a group of radio engineers in Princeton, New Jersey. ''My topic was space,'' he later wrote, ''so I thought it would be interesting to make some calculations concerning the possibilities of communications satellites. I was astounded at the way things looked when I actually made the calculations.'' Pierce presented three possibilities: a satellite in a low earth orbit that would, like a mirror, reflect signals bounced against it; a satellite orbiting at about the same height that would actively receive, amplify and rebroadcast signals; and a similar satellite in a geostationary orbit.

Without ever having read or heard about Clarke's article in *Wireless World,* Pierce came to many of the conclusions that the young radar instructor had published a decade earlier. ''I did not regard what I had done as an invention,'' Pierce said many years later. ''I regarded it as something that everyone must have thought of. That may seem rather odd, but it seemed to me an inevitable idea.''

Less than a year after speaking to the convention, Pierce published his findings in *Jet Propulsion,* the journal of the American Rocket Society. In contrast to the general silence that greeted Clarke, Pierce's ideas were received with

enthusiasm, not least because many of the missing pieces needed to build and operate satellites had since become available. Transistors, invented in 1948, were replacing heavy, short-lived and power-hungry vacuum tubes. Solar cells, which produce electricity directly from sunlight, offered a ready supply of electrical energy. In the field of microwave communications, new supersensitive receivers and powerful amplifiers called masers (for "microwave amplification by stimulated emission of radiation") had been developed to handle the faint signals that would emanate from space.

Most important, rocketry was developing much faster than had been expected. In the mid-1950s, although a satellite in geostationary orbit remained but a distant goal, putting artificial moons in low orbit became a reality. Then, in 1957 the Soviet Union launched *Sputnik,* surging ahead in the race for space. Determined to recapture the lead, the United States put its own space effort into high gear.

In 1958, Pierce and Rudi Kompfner, a colleague at Bell Labs, read about plans of the National Aeronautics and Space Administration to orbit a huge, shiny balloon. By tracking it, NASA scientists were hoping to learn about the density of the earth's upper atmosphere. Pierce and Kompfner immediately recognized a perfect opportunity to test Pierce's theory about a reflecting satellite in low earth orbit. They approached NASA with the idea, and the space agency agreed to cooperate.

On August 12, 1960, a Delta rocket carried the inflatable satellite, named

Echo I, into a circular orbit. The balloon was folded neatly into a 27-inch magnesium container, which split in half after entering orbit to release the satellite. Chemical compounds sprinkled inside *Echo I* before the launch evaporated in the vacuum of space, causing the satellite to expand to its full 100-foot diameter. Using earth stations built specially for the project, Bell and NASA researchers successfully bounced voice, music and data signals off *Echo I* from one side of the United States to the other. *Echo I's* aluminized skin also made it highly visible in the night sky, and newspapers told their readers when it would appear and where in the sky to look for it.

The success of *Echo I* and some early military satellites — which received signals beamed from earth, recorded the information on magnetic tape, then retransmitted the signals to other earth stations as they came within range — fired the imaginations of engineers at Bell Labs. As outlined by Pierce, the logical next step in satellite technology would be to orbit a satellite that relayed messages as soon as it received them. That satellite would eventually be *Telstar*.

BRINGING THE SATELLITE TO LIFE

Building *Telstar* presented a formidable technical challenge for the scientists and engineers at Bell Labs, requiring more people than Bell had ever assigned to work on a single project. But AT&T knew that the stakes were high. Like microwaves, communications satellites had the potential to encroach upon Bell's long-distance business. By demonstrating technical mastery of the field, AT&T hoped to lay early claim to the new technology.

Even before *Telstar* was launched in 1962, AT&T had drawn up plans for an international communications system using a swarm of satellites like *Telstar* in low earth orbits. Each one would have an elliptical orbit with a perigee, or closest approach to the earth, of about 500 miles and an apogee, or farthest point from the earth, of about 3,000 miles above the Atlantic Ocean. Only near the apogee would a satellite be ideally positioned to relay signals between Europe and Maine, and that arrangement lasted at best for only half an hour or so, three or four times a day. Thus, for round-the-clock transmissions, 30 or more satellites would be needed.

At the time, *Telstar* was a marvel of mechanical ingenuity and miniaturization. The satellite's full complement of electronics fit into an aluminum drum 20 inches tall and less than three feet wide. Liquid polyurethane foam, poured around each electronic subassembly in the canister, solidified into a shock-absorbent foam to cushion *Telstar's* transistors and diodes. The canister itself, instead of being bolted to the satellite framework, was suspended inside by a web of nylon cords to reduce shock even more. To regulate *Telstar's* internal temperature as the satellite passed from sunlight into darkness, a thermostatically controlled door opened or closed as necessary to maintain just the right amount of heat generated by the vehicle's electronics.

The earth station at Andover was to be a prototype of the earth stations that would be used to track and communicate with the satellites. As a result, no expense was spared in making Andover a showpiece of the new technology. Its 380-ton horn antenna was the largest of its kind ever built. To intercept the satellite's faint transmissions, it had a square aperture with sides 60 feet long. Precision drive mechanisms, slowly turning the antenna a small fraction of an inch at a time, kept the aperture aimed continuously at the satellite as it passed from horizon to horizon.

To protect the antenna from wind, rain and the harsh New England winters, it was covered by a dome made of rubberized fabric. Air pressure, held slightly higher inside the dome than the atmospheric pressure outside, inflated the antenna's shield to a spherical shape. At 210 feet in diameter, the dome was also the largest of its kind. For the most part, the dome did its job well, but it was not immune to mishaps. One winter, a slushy snowfall made a large dimple in the center of the dome, pushing the fabric toward the fragile antenna underneath. As planned, the heating system started to melt the snow, but that only exchanged one problem for another by creating a small lake on top of the dome. In the end, an enterprising employee fired a few shots from a rifle through the fabric, allowing the water to drain away safely. As the lake became a puddle, the air pressure inside the dome overcame the dimple and popped the shield back into place, causing a slushy avalanche to cascade down the dome's side and demolish a nearby trailer.

Telstar was a triumph for Bell Labs and a hit with the public. A romantic tune of the same name topped the popular music charts for three weeks in 1962. In Rome, a corner newspaper vendor named his kiosk Telstar. For several years thereafter, all communications satellites were known as telstars. Yet this spectacular demonstration of AT&T's prowess in space failed to secure for the company any lasting advantage in satellite communications. A month after *Telstar's* launch, the U.S. Congress, which had been debating the issue of whether space should be open to private enterprise, passed the 1962 Communications Satellite Act. The act instituted a quasi-private company called the Communications Satellite Corporation (Comsat), owned half by common carriers—AT&T, Western Union, RCA and a few others—and half by the general public. The legislation endowed Comsat alone with the right to establish international communications by satellite. Though AT&T would play a part in developing satellites through its partial ownership of Comsat, it could not take the lead. Bell Labs began winding down its satellite effort, and eventually AT&T sold even the Andover earth station to Comsat.

THE GEOSTATIONARY OPTION

Well before *Telstar's* success, some communications experts were already convinced that low earth orbits like *Telstar's* were a waste of effort. They pointed to the many advantages of the geostationary orbit first cited by Clarke, including the ease of tracking and broad coverage of the earth. Though existing rockets were not yet powerful enough to reach such an orbit, they argued that it was shortsighted to pursue low earth orbits with rocketry advancing so rapidly.

Among the earliest of these believers were three engineers at the Hughes Aircraft Company: Harold Rosen, Donald Williams and Thomas Hudspeth. In 1959 they began designing a communications satellite weighing so little that it could be launched into geostationary orbit on rockets that would soon be available. To reduce the power needed for the satellite's signal, they figured out a way to stabilize the satellite so that the gaze of its antenna would never wander from earth. They also designed an on-board rocket system that could gently nudge the satellite back into place when it strayed from its assigned spot in the sky.

89

Relaying Microwave Transmissions

Any electromagnetic wave with a frequency between one GHZ (gigahertz, or billion hertz) and 300 GHZ may be defined as a microwave, but the frequencies commonly used in communications range from two to 40 GHZ. At these frequencies, signals are easily focused into highly directional beams; lower-frequency radio waves, in contrast, propagate in all directions from an antenna. Microwaves are thus suited to point-to-point transmission, and the narrow beams make it possible to operate many microwave circuits in a small region without mutual interference. A system of repeater stations (right, below) can relay microwave transmissions overland; satellites can relay them over longer distances.

Because of the directionality of the signal, microwave communication requires line-of-sight contact. Terrestrial repeater stations cannot be hidden from one another by obstacles such as buildings or by the curvature of the earth; typically, such stations are located 20 to 30 miles apart. A satellite, with a large part of the earth's surface in its line of sight, can communicate virtually simultaneously with many ground stations. If it is in geostationary orbit (below), it can maintain constant line-of-sight contact. In other orbits, satellites rise and set and can communicate with ground stations only at certain times.

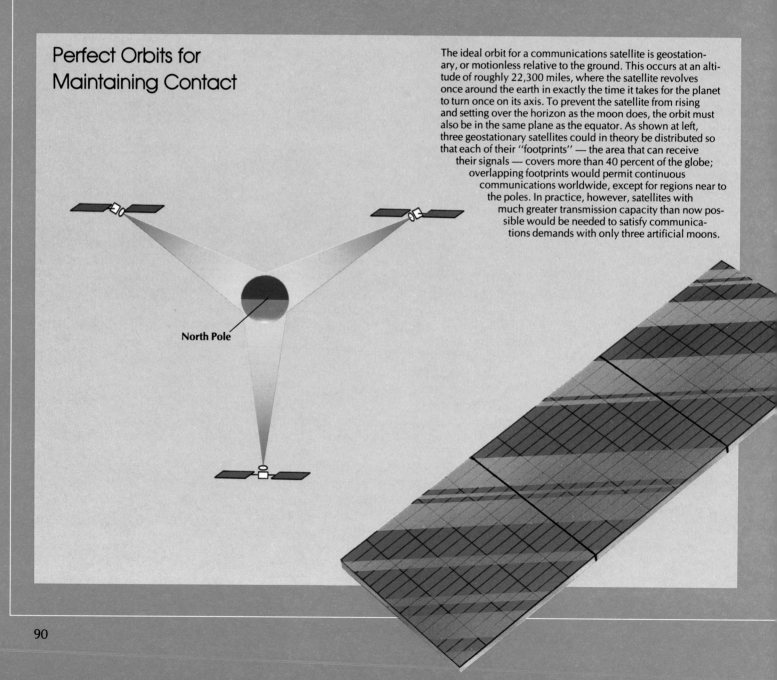

Perfect Orbits for Maintaining Contact

The ideal orbit for a communications satellite is geostationary, or motionless relative to the ground. This occurs at an altitude of roughly 22,300 miles, where the satellite revolves once around the earth in exactly the time it takes for the planet to turn once on its axis. To prevent the satellite from rising and setting over the horizon as the moon does, the orbit must also be in the same plane as the equator. As shown at left, three geostationary satellites could in theory be distributed so that each of their "footprints" — the area that can receive their signals — covers more than 40 percent of the globe; overlapping footprints would permit continuous communications worldwide, except for regions near to the poles. In practice, however, satellites with much greater transmission capacity than now possible would be needed to satisfy communications demands with only three artificial moons.

North Pole

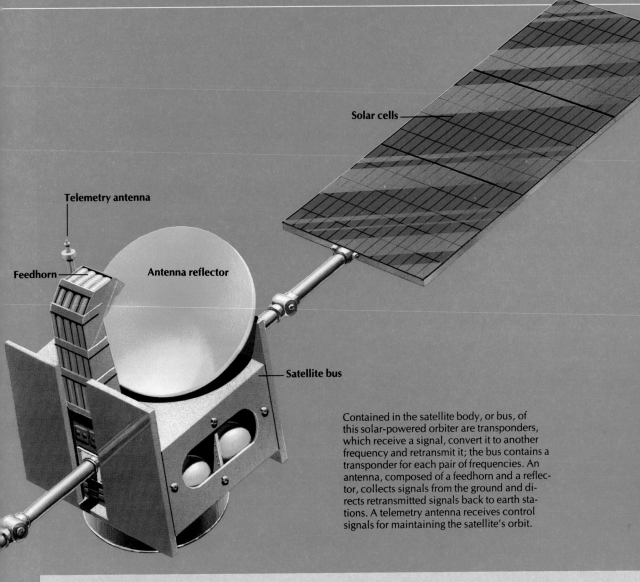

Solar cells

Telemetry antenna

Feedhorn

Antenna reflector

Satellite bus

Contained in the satellite body, or bus, of this solar-powered orbiter are transponders, which receive a signal, convert it to another frequency and retransmit it; the bus contains a transponder for each pair of frequencies. An antenna, composed of a feedhorn and a reflector, collects signals from the ground and directs retransmitted signals back to earth stations. A telemetry antenna receives control signals for maintaining the satellite's orbit.

Terrestrial Microwave Links

In this full-duplex (two-way simultaneous) digital microwave communications system, point-to-point transmissions link two voice and data networks. One network digitizes a message, modulates it onto a specific frequency, and transmits it to the first repeater station. The station regenerates the signal to compensate for attenuation, then retransmits to the next repeater station. When the signal reaches the other network, it is converted back into a voice or data message.

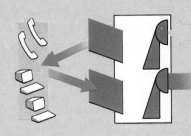
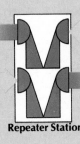
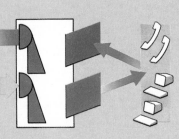

Repeater Station

Sending and Receiving Messages via Satellite

Satellite communications systems employ several techniques to allow one satellite to relay signals to and from more than one earth station at a time without signal interference. Typically, satellites carry several transponders that operate at different frequencies, each corresponding to an earth station (or a set of stations) tuned to that frequency.

Another method, illustrated here, is called TDMA (time-division multiple access), which works in a manner similar to the time-division multiplexing used in land-based networks

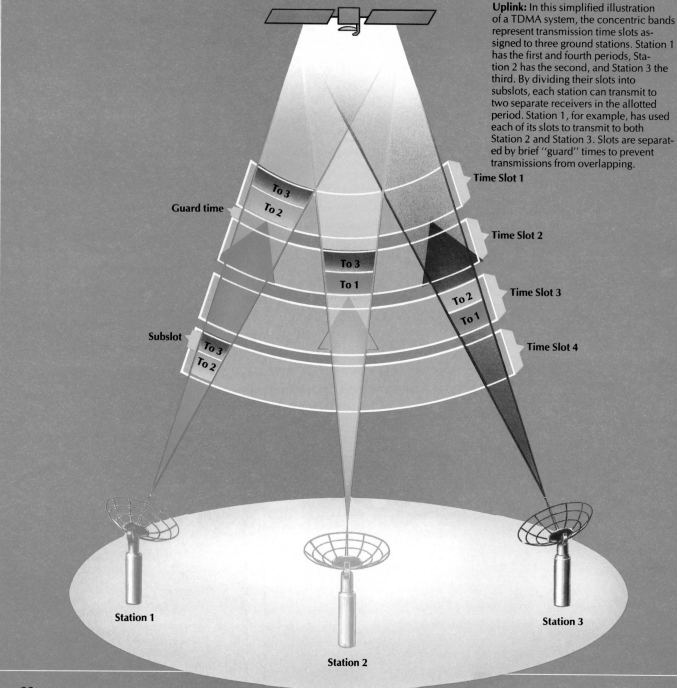

Uplink: In this simplified illustration of a TDMA system, the concentric bands represent transmission time slots assigned to three ground stations. Station 1 has the first and fourth periods, Station 2 has the second, and Station 3 the third. By dividing their slots into subslots, each station can transmit to two separate receivers in the allotted period. Station 1, for example, has used each of its slots to transmit to both Station 2 and Station 3. Slots are separated by brief "guard" times to prevent transmissions from overlapping.

Time Slot 1

Time Slot 2

Time Slot 3

Time Slot 4

To 3
To 2

Guard time

To 3
To 1

To 2
To 1

Subslot

To 3
To 2

Station 1

Station 2

Station 3

(pages 32-33). Transmission takes the form of a series of frames, usually 2 milliseconds in length. Each frame is divided into as many as 35 slots. Assigned a particular slot within each frame — the second slot, say, or the fifth and seventh — ground stations divide their messages into short signal bursts, sending a burst every time the appropriate slot opens up on the system's transmission schedule; a master station synchronizes the system by providing a reference burst at the beginning of each frame. Because the satellite retransmits all incoming signals, ground stations pick up transmissions intended for them according to their assigned time slots.

Some satellites, operating at higher frequencies, can effectively double their capacity by using the same frequency for separate transmissions; they simply transmit the narrow-beam signals in different directions. These systems often employ a more complex technique known as satellite-switched TDMA to transmit messages between ground stations in different footprints.

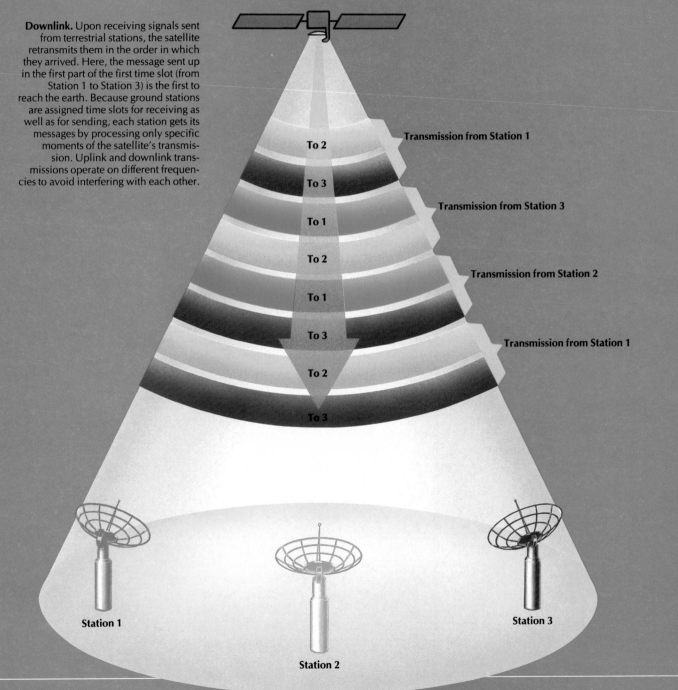

Downlink. Upon receiving signals sent from terrestrial stations, the satellite retransmits them in the order in which they arrived. Here, the message sent up in the first part of the first time slot (from Station 1 to Station 3) is the first to reach the earth. Because ground stations are assigned time slots for receiving as well as for sending, each station gets its messages by processing only specific moments of the satellite's transmission. Uplink and downlink transmissions operate on different frequencies to avoid interfering with each other.

To 2

To 3

To 1

To 2

To 1

To 3

To 2

To 3

Transmission from Station 1

Transmission from Station 3

Transmission from Station 2

Transmission from Station 1

Station 1

Station 2

Station 3

One big problem remained: The engineers had to convince their managers that the project was worth taking on. Unlike AT&T, Hughes had no intention of assuming the entire expense of building, launching and operating a communications satellite, and the company was initially unable to persuade NASA to back the project. But the three engineers pleaded that they at least be allowed to begin building the satellite. Ultimately, a frustrated Williams went to a vice president of the company and laid a check for $10,000 on his desk. "Here's what I want to contribute to the program," he said. "I'm sorry, it's all I can do." The company refused his money, but the gesture was enough to turn the tide: Hughes gave their engineers the go-ahead.

In 1962, NASA finally agreed to take a chance on the project, and early the next year *Syncom I* blasted into space. It reached geostationary orbit, but its electronics refused to work once it arrived. *Syncoms II* and *III* succeeded in relaying messages, but because they were sponsored by the military, they had little effect on commercial communications. The launch that really initiated the age of geostationary communications satellites was that of Comsat's *Early Bird,* the fourth in the series, rocketed spaceward in April 1965. Lyndon Johnson, by then president of the United States, used the satellite to address Europe on the 20th anniversary of V-E Day. Doctors in Geneva watched as heart surgeon Michael DeBakey operated on a patient in the U.S. Most important, with the launching of *Early Bird,* the number of telephone links between America and Europe, previously available only by undersea cable, immediately increased by more than a third.

BURGEONING CAPACITY

Since the launch of *Early Bird,* the use of satellites for international communications has expanded dramatically. Whereas *Early Bird* had a maximum capacity of 240 voice circuits, the most recent international communications satellites have 15,000, and the next generation will have eight times that number. Computer data also travels over the same circuits, since modems make it possible for data to go anywhere a telephone call can go.

Even though domestic communications traffic usually exceeds international traffic, nearly a decade elapsed between *Early Bird* and the first U.S. satellite intended for domestic communications. At the outset it appeared that satellites could not compete economically with terrestrial microwave networks, such as those operated by MCI and other companies. But as experience with international satellites accumulated, and as the costs of satellites and earth stations dropped, the economics of domestic satellites became more appealing. Then regulatory disputes intervened. Comsat claimed that it should be granted the exclusive right to build and operate such satellites because of its international charter from Congress. But the Communications Satellite Act did not definitively address the issue of domestic satellites, and other companies protested. Finally, in 1972, the FCC issued what is known as its "open skies" decision. Any company would be permitted to send up a satellite as long as the enterprise met the FCC's licensing requirements.

In 1974, Western Union became the first company to put a domestic communications satellite, named *Westar,* into geostationary orbit. Shortly thereafter, RCA, AT&T and General Telephone and Electric all launched their own communications spacecraft, and today a variety of corporate and government satellites are parked in the Clarke belt.

The predominant forms of traffic to and from these orbiting relay stations remain voice and especially video signals. Yet the demand for data transmissions is growing much more quickly than is the demand for conventional voice and video services. Moreover, data transmissions have had a disproportionate effect on the way satellites have evolved.

A QUARTER-SECOND HICCUP
In sending data by satellite, several considerations come into play that pose no difficulties for group-based networks. Perhaps most important is signal delay. Geostationary satellites are so far from the earth — about a tenth of the way to the moon — that a signal takes nearly a quarter of a second to travel from the earth to the satellite and back. This delay makes some techniques used for overland computer communications highly inefficient when used with satellites. For instance, with stop-and-wait error control, a computer transmits a block of data and then asks for confirmation that the data was correctly received. Such procedures would slow the satellite data transmission rate to a crawl. Special transmission protocols have been developed that greatly reduce the inefficiencies caused by signal delay. But they often require expensive software or additional hardware, and because of their special features, they are ill suited for overland data communications. Consequently, data is often transmitted by satellite using one kind of protocol, then switched to another protocol for cross-country distribution.

Balancing the problems of signal delay are several advantages to sending computer data by way of satellite. One of the most basic involves a trend that has affected much more than just satellites — the increasing digitization of the communications network. Traditionally, signals have traveled through the communications system in analog form. Even digital computer signals have customarily been translated into their analog equivalents by modems before traveling over telephone lines.

Recently, however, communications companies have begun to explore the benefits of sending signals in digital form. Any time a signal travels a great distance, it fades and must periodically be strengthened. This is one function of repeater towers for microwaves, and of satellites for space-based communications. With analog signals, repeaters have no way to distinguish between the information a signal is carrying and the noise it has picked up during its travels. Repeaters, therefore, unavoidably amplify the noise along with the information. But the bits of data in a digital signal stand out as discrete pulses against background noise, permitting a repeater to ignore the noise and retransmit the data in very nearly its original form.

The economies of moving data in digital form have become more and more attractive. Microchips can handle the complex tasks involved in reshaping, switching and otherwise processing digital signals much more efficiently and cheaply than conventional equipment can handle analog signals. As a result, telephone companies increasingly have been converting analog signals — including voice and video signals — into their digital equivalents, then sending those signals over transmission lines equipped to send data in digital form.

It is no simple task to convert land-based analog networks entirely to digital transmission. Over the decades, billions of dollars have been invested in analog equipment; replacing this vast infrastructure with digital apparatus will take a number of years. But satellites are not subject to this constraint. When designing a satellite system, a company can opt for digital transmission from the start. It was just such a decision that laid the groundwork for one of the most interesting corporate ventures in the history of satellite communications.

IBM'S ENTRY INTO SPACE

In 1974, IBM asked the FCC's approval for a joint venture it had planned with Comsat. The purpose was to provide a satellite communications system for businesses. The network would handle voice, video and data transmissions in an all-digital format, using sophisticated computers on the ground to route and process messages. Customers would own and operate their own earth stations with roof-top antennas for sending and receiving satellite signals, thus bypassing the telephone system completely.

AT&T, as might be expected, protested vigorously. But IBM's proposal also alarmed other companies in the data-processing community, which saw the move as an attempt by IBM to establish dominance in data communications as well as data processing. With an extensive communications system geared exclusively to its own equipment, IBM could create a virtual monopoly in satellite communications for businesses and lock out other firms from this potentially lucrative market.

In response to these concerns, the FCC imposed a number of conditions on the proposal. It required that IBM set up a separate subsidiary to handle its part of the project. The regulators also insisted that IBM and Comsat include another partner in the venture, which they promptly did in the form of Aetna Life and Casualty, the insurance company.

Perhaps IBM's competition need not have worried so much about the venture's prospects. The resulting company, called Satellite Business Services, was a risky undertaking from the outset. SBS expected at first to snare little of the voice and video business already going to such telecommunications services as AT&T and MCI. Instead, it planned to attract the large companies it saw as potential customers by offering services that were, in the mid-1970s, new and innovative: electronic mail, teleconferencing and high-speed data transmission. Success would depend on changing some of the ways that companies traditionally did business. For instance, they would have to be sold on the idea of holding conferences by satellite rather than flying their executives to meetings. SBS planners realized that marketing their wares would be one of their greatest challenges.

The task turned out to be every bit as demanding as anticipated. Regulatory delays postponed the beginning of service until 1981. By that time, SBS had lined up fewer than two dozen customers. Businesses simply did not seem ready for the services that SBS had to offer. Before long, the company was hundreds of millions of dollars in debt. SBS restructured its offering to emphasize conventional voice and video transmissions, but its losses continued to mount.

In 1984 Comsat became the first of the three partners to pull out, citing its need to conserve cash for other projects. Then in 1985, in a complicated deal, IBM bought out Aetna and sold SBS to a competitor, MCI. At the same time, IBM bought 18 percent of MCI, with an eye toward buying more of the company in the future. IBM had given up its satellite business but had secured something it wanted even more: a continued presence in the telecommunications field.

Meanwhile, the regulatory fetters on AT&T had been loosened as a result of an unprecedented corporate breakup ordered in 1982. In essence, the company gave up ownership of the 22 regional Bell telephone companies around the nation, which had been the major part of the corporation. In return, AT&T was allowed to compete in an arena formerly barred to it—data processing. Thus AT&T and IBM maneuvered themselves into positions where they compete head to head, not only in data processing but in data communications as well. Nowhere else is the convergence of telecommunications and computing more apparent than in the rivalry between these two corporate giants.

HYBRID SERVICES

Even in failing, SBS made use of several innovations in satellite communications. Smaller earth stations are a prime example. As the hard of hearing once resorted to ear trumpets, earth stations once required antennas of enormous dimensions to capture as much as possible of the faint signals produced by early communications satellites. In addition, each station cost millions of dollars to build and operate. But as satellite signals became more powerful, the size of earth-station antennas decreased proportionately. Also, the computers that managed earth-station operations declined in price along with other kinds of data-processing equipment. By the time of the SBS debut, an earth-station antenna could be as small as 16 feet in diameter, and the cost of the complete facility averaged $345,000.

Earth stations can be very inexpensive indeed if they are intended only to receive satellite signals, thus saving the cost of a transmitter. In the 1970s, several companies began experimenting with small, receive-only earth stations. Muzak Corporation, for example, adopted one-way earth stations for distributing the music that fills restaurants and stores. A few years later, homeowners began to buy receive-only earth stations to intercept television signals relayed by satellite.

One entrepreneur who early on recognized the appeal of bargain-priced earth stations was Edwin Parker. A communications professor at Stanford University, Parker quit his teaching job in 1979, founded a company named Equatorial Earth Stations, and soon thereafter introduced a receive-only antenna a mere two feet in diameter. Moreover, at $2,500, the total cost of the system was just 60 percent of the cost of acquiring the same information over telephone lines. Within three years, Equatorial had sold 20,000 of the dishes to such companies as Reuters news service and Dow Jones, a large provider of financial information in the United States.

With the proliferation of small earth stations able to receive data from the Clarke belt, more and more companies began offering information by satellite. Especially popular have been large, quickly changing data bases, such as financial information, news, weather reports—and even betting odds. Those who provide these services assert that transmitting data by satellite is cheaper, less susceptible to error and more flexible than sending it over land-based networks.

When two-way communication is required—to acknowledge that data has arrived without error, to request retransmission in case of an error or to ask for one of several options offered by a data-base service—the receiver must also be able

A Network Made of Skeins of Glass

Increasingly, the world's communications systems are being knit together by hairlike fibers that can transmit tremendous volumes of digitized information as pulses of light. The source of light may be either a light-emitting diode (LED) or a laser, as shown in the photograph at left; in either case, electrical signals, such as those from a telephone, are converted to pulses of light. LEDs emit up to 200 million pulses, or bits, per second over short distances. Commercially available lasers can generate as many as 1.7 billion pulses per second — about 24,000 typical phone conversations — a rate that has doubled annually in recent years. At the receiving end, a photodetector

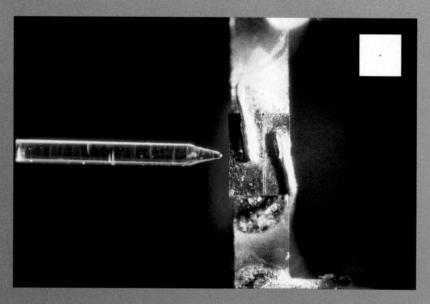

Two elements of a fiber-optics system — a light-emitting laser and a single fiber — are shown at left approximately 50 times life size. To capture the laser's beam most effectively, the end of the fiber is formed into a lens, which varies from blunt to pointed depending on the manufacturer. The fiber measures 125 micrometers, or millionths of a meter, across; the laser (the rectangular chip containing two electrical connectors) is 500 micrometers on its long side. At 25,400 micrometers to an inch, this makes the laser roughly the size of a grain of salt (red dot at upper right).

cladding

core

coating

The outer coating of an optical fiber protects a cylindrical core and its surrounding cladding from the environment. It also prevents light from fibers bundled together in a cable from interfering with one another's signals.

senses the light pulses and translates them back into electrical signals to be routed to the receiving telephone.

In between, the light travels along the fiber, which is designed to confine the light to the interior and allow it to follow the fiber's path — even around corners. This seemingly impossible feat is achieved by manipulating the so-called refractive indices of fiber-optic materials. Refraction is the deflection from a straight path of a light ray as it passes obliquely from one medium (such as air) into another (such as glass) in which the speed of light is different; the mathematical relationship between light's speed through a given material and its velocity in a vacuum is the material's refractive index. The higher a material's refractive index, the slower light travels through it.

In an optical fiber, a central core of glass is surrounded by so-called cladding (cutaway), a similar material with a lower refractive index; light pulsed through the fiber will be bent at the interface toward the material with the higher refractive index — the core. As illustrated below, the diameter of the core and the difference between the refractive indices of core and cladding determine the clarity of the signal received at the other end of an optical fiber.

Keeping Light on the Straight and Narrow

The three types of optical fibers diagramed here illustrate the principles employed to guide light long distances without loss of information. Step-index fibers (top) are characterized by a sharp transition of refractive index at the boundary between the core and the cladding; in graded-index fibers (middle), the index of refraction is highest in the center of the core and tapers gradually to a lower value in the cladding. As shown here, both of these schemes employ a large-diameter core, which allows multiple modes — groups of rays that enter and reflect through the fiber at different angles; because some rays travel longer paths than others, the received signal is distorted to some extent. Single-mode fibers (bottom) feature a step index but the core of the fiber is very small, thus allowing the propagation of only one light ray and a virtually distortion-free signal.

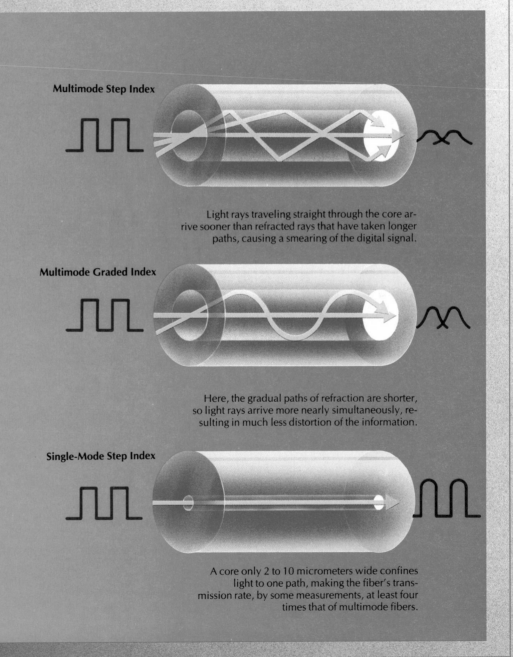

Multimode Step Index

Light rays traveling straight through the core arrive sooner than refracted rays that have taken longer paths, causing a smearing of the digital signal.

Multimode Graded Index

Here, the gradual paths of refraction are shorter, so light rays arrive more nearly simultaneously, resulting in much less distortion of the information.

Single-Mode Step Index

A core only 2 to 10 micrometers wide confines light to one path, making the fiber's transmission rate, by some measurements, at least four times that of multimode fibers.

to transmit. In some cases, computers receive data from satellites and transmit requests and replies over conventional phone lines. But two-way communication by satellite has also become affordable. In 1984, Equatorial Earth Stations introduced a line of four-foot antennas capable of transmitting as well as receiving and costing less than $6,000; a number of competitors have followed suit.

The surge toward satellite communications has raised the specter of a colossal signal jam. Many satellite links operate on the same frequencies as earthbound microwave communications systems, and with a limited number of channels available, congestion was becoming a problem in urban areas even before the advent of inexpensive earth stations. When a company or common carrier wants to establish a new microwave link in a major city, months may pass before a path free of interference is found. Switching to higher frequencies, where congestion is less severe, can offer some relief, but only if a decrease in reliability is acceptable. Microwaves above 10 billion hertz can be blocked by heavy rainfall.

Satellites themselves also suffer from congestion. Geostationary satellites can be placed no closer together than 1,000 miles or their signals interfere with one another, and already some segments of the Clarke belt are filled. In recent years, negotiations on the international allotment of slots for geostationary satellites have become acrimonious and will probably become more heated as developing countries seek to orbit satellites of their own.

Fortunately, satellites are not the only transmission medium capable of carrying tomorrow's communications. A new technology, advancing with much promise, may eventually supplant satellites as the method of choice for transmitting all kinds of information, from television pictures to computer data. In some ways, it is a technology reminiscent of an earlier age in telecommunications, relying on cables rather than microwaves or orbiting relay stations. There the similarities stop, however, for these cables are made not of copper wires but of filaments of the purest glass.

COMMUNICATING BY LIGHT BEAM

The idea of using glass as a communications medium grew out of a remarkable invention: a new form of light. In 1958, Charles Townes of Columbia University and Arthur Schawlow of Bell Labs described how to make a beam of light that contained rays of a single frequency. They drew their inspiration from a phenomenon, first described by Albert Einstein, that found earlier application in the maser. The amount of energy in a molecule can be increased by heating it or by bathing it in light of a particular frequency. When light of a different frequency passes nearby, it triggers the molecule to surrender some of this energy in the form of additional light rays having the same wavelength as the trigger and traveling in precisely the same direction. The new rays pass near other molecules, releasing yet more light, quickly increasing the intensity of beam. Townes and Schawlow called this process "light amplification by stimulated emission of radiation." Shortened to "laser," the name eventually came to mean the equipment necessary to produce such a beam. The first operating lasers were demonstrated in 1960 by research teams at Hughes Research Laboratories and Bell Labs. By the mid-1980s, hundreds of thousands of lasers had found application in fields ranging from surgery to welding.

From the laser's first appearance, engineers realized that the device had the potential to be a virtuoso of communications. Instead of the helter-skelter disarray of light waves produced by other sources, lasers generate a beam in which the waves parallel one another, like columns of well-drilled soldiers. This coherency, as it is called, greatly enhances light's ability to serve as an information-carrying medium, and made possible for the first time a narrow, intense beam that could travel great distances with little widening and consequent loss of intensity. With frequencies 100,000 times higher than those of microwaves, the spectrum of visible light possesses the staggering potential capacity to carry 80 million television channels.

There was one problem to solve before light could fulfill this promise. Even more than high-frequency microwaves, light beams are impeded and scattered by atmospheric obstacles: rain, clouds, dust or smog. A conduit for conveying the beams from point to point would have to be found.

One of the people to begin thinking about this problem was Charles Kuen Kao, an electrical engineer born in China and educated in England who was working at the research laboratories of International Telephone & Telegraph just outside London. He had been studying ways of sending microwaves down hollow pipes called waveguides. To Kao it seemed that there ought to be a similar way to transmit light along enclosed passages. For a while, he considered sending light down hollow tubes, with mirrors or lenses to bend the light around corners. But such tubes would have to follow perfectly straight paths for much of their length, and they promised to be difficult to install, just as waveguides were.

THE POTENTIAL OF GLASS
Kao was also familiar with the bundles of glass filaments, or optical fibers, then being used in industry and medicine to convey light into hard-to-reach places. These fibers had a core of one kind of glass surrounded by glass of another kind that redirected light toward the center of the core whenever it strayed to the edges. Theoretically, laser light could carry messages along these fibers. But light dissipated in them so quickly that the signal would have required repeaters every few yards, an impractical arrangement for communications. The unit "decibel per meter" is used to measure how much of the light signal's strength is lost for every meter of transmission; even the best fibers then in existence had losses in excess of 1,000 decibels per kilometer. By another calculation, a light signal dwindled to less than 1 percent of its original strength in traveling through as little as 10 meters of fiber. "Glass fiber was not a very strong contender in the beginning," Kao later recalled, "people didn't believe that the losses could be reduced."

But Kao did not give up on fibers. He and a colleague, G. A. Hockham, began to study the factors that make light fade in glass. They found that minuscule quantities of water and certain metals were the culprits. In a landmark paper published in 1966, they demonstrated theoretically that no law of nature stood in the way of dramatically reducing these impurities: It should be possible to make an optical fiber that can transmit light with losses as low as 20 decibels per kilometer. If that could be done, repeaters could be separated by miles rather than yards, and optical-fiber communications would be feasible.

To meet the challenge posed by Kao and Hockham, glassmakers had to improve the clarity of their product a billion times. The first company to achieve that goal was Corning Glass Works of Corning, New York. They pioneered a method of evenly depositing particles of silica, the main constituent of glass, around a ceramic rod. The first layers of particles contained infinitesimal amounts of carefully chosen impurities — germanium, boron or phosphorus — intended to change the material's refractive index (page 99); these layers would form the core of an optical fiber when the process was complete. Subsequent layers, which would become the fiber's cladding, were pure silica. The intermediate result was a tube of deposits a couple of inches in diameter and, though composed of tiny particles, firm enough for the ceramic rod to be removed from the center. Next, the deposits were heated to fuse them into a glass tube that was gradually transformed into a solid rod, which was then drawn into a fiber.

Since this breakthrough, researchers have developed a number of other ways to make optical fibers. By the mid-1980s, glass fibers had become so clear that they could transmit more than 95 percent of the light they received for a distance of a kilometer. If the world's oceans were that clear, a person traveling over the deepest waters of the Pacific — the 32,000-foot-deep Marianas Trench — could easily see the sea floor.

LIGHT-PULSES BY THE BILLIONS
Even as Kao and Hockham were thinking about optical fibers, other engineers were developing lasers no larger than a grain of salt that would eventually shine light through them. These tiny lasers can be turned on and off to emit billions of pulses of light per second. In conjunction with optical fibers, this on-off mode of operation is ideal for conveying digital information, the presence of light corresponding to a one, its absence signifying a zero. Using such a scheme, an optical fiber can transmit the entire Encyclopaedia Britannica in less than five seconds.

The huge capacity and digital proficiency of optical fibers have made them a natural for computer communications. They are being used in local area networks to connect central processors with peripheral equipment and other computers, creating integrated computer systems that span a room, a building, a campus or a city. Developers are incorporating data highways made of optical fibers into the design of skyscrapers; intelligent buildings, as they are called, have nervous systems of optical fibers that carry information about temperatures, lighting, breaches of security or fire alarms to a central computer for action.

Two kinds of optical fiber vie for supremacy in the communications marketplace — multimode fibers and single-mode fibers. Multimode fibers have a relatively thick core of glass, which makes them less expensive to manufacture and easier to align when lengths of fiber are spliced together. Another advantage of multimode fibers is that they do not require a laser light source; comparatively economical light-emitting diodes, most familiar as the bright, red numbers displayed by early electronic calculators and digital watches, are perfectly suitable.

But the thick core also limits the capacity of such fibers. Because of the width of the core, light pulses, which are each composed of many rays, travel down a multimode fiber something like a handful of marbles thrown along a sewer pipe. Some of the rays might reach the end of the core without touching the sides; others carom wildly from one side of the core to another. Because light that bounces off the sides of the core travels farther than light that goes directly down its center, pulses of light lose definition as they progress along a multimode fiber.

The pulses therefore must be separated enough not to overlap, which limits both the number of pulses per second that can be sent down this kind of fiber and how far they may travel before requiring regeneration, the process of restoring definition to the light pulses.

In a single-mode fiber, the glass core is extraordinarily narrow. The rays of a light pulse, therefore, have little space to bounce from side to side. As a result, the pulses of light retain their definition, permitting as many as 30 times the number of pulses per second to be transmitted through a single-mode fiber as through the multimode variety. For the same reason, pulses can travel much farther in a single-mode fiber before the signal requires regeneration. The lessened demand for expensive regenerators more than compensates for the extra cost of buying and installing single-mode fibers and the premium paid for laser light sources, which the narrow core in this type of fiber requires.

Both multimode and single-mode fibers have several steps on conventional copper wires, in addition to their huge information-carrying capacity. Stray electromagnetic impulses do not affect glass as they do wires, so optical fibers are immune to errors in data caused by electrical interference. Thus, they are ideally suited for use in places like machine shops and factories, where conventional wires often require shielding. Furthermore, optical fibers offer tight security because they are extremely difficult to tap, making them attractive for military as well as banking applications. Fiber-optic cables are much smaller and lighter than copper-wire cables, one reason why telephone companies have begun to install them in cities, where they can snake through conduits crowded almost to capacity.

TOWARD A DIGITAL FUTURE

Optical fibers have progressed to the point that they need fewer repeaters than do twisted-pair wires or coaxial cables. Consequently, even though fibers remain somewhat more expensive than wire, they are fully competitive with it in almost all long-distance applications. This economic argument in favor of fibers has not been lost on the telephone companies. They have already installed hundreds of thousands of miles of optical fibers into their existing transmission grids, and fiber optics are being used in more than 20 countries. In a few years, fiber-optic cables will be carrying messages between the United States and Europe, and cables beneath the Pacific will follow shortly. Some experts have even predicted that undersea optical fibers will begin taking so much business away from international communications satellites that few will be launched for commercial purposes in the 1990s.

But these changes are just the beginning of the fiber-optics revolution. By the mid-1980s, communications specialists had already begun to think in terms of a single, unified communications grid tying together every business, household and computer within a country and eventually throughout the world. They call it ISDN — the Integrated Services Digital Network.

According to its proponents, an ISDN could carry all of the information that someday might flow into or out of a home or business — computer services, voice transmissions, and possibly even television and radio signals. It represents the ultimate integration of telecommunications, replacing the many separate networks used today to carry voice, video and data signals. Such a variety of services would probably require the high capacity of optical fibers to become a reality. But an ISDN can also be implemented on a more limited scale with older technologies. Small-scale ISDN experiments using wire connections have been conducted in several European countries.

If fiber optics are used to set up future ISDNs, one of the most difficult parts of the transition will be stringing the local loops — the lines between neighborhood exchange offices and individual homes or businesses. Connecting one of these circuits to another to complete a telephone call or receive a favorite television program depends on switches at the local exchange, and switching technology has been a weak point of fiber-optics communications systems. Before a signal carried by optical fibers can be switched electronically — the only means available for the immediate future — its information must be converted from light into electrical signals. Electronic switches usually have less capacity than optical fibers, making them a bottleneck for the system. Researchers are working on so-called optical switches, which use the properties of certain materials to direct light signals from one place to another without converting them to electricity. But such switches are not expected to be perfected before the 1990s.

A more immediate problem involves establishing standards for future ISDNs. In 1980, the CCITT began issuing a partial set of such standards, but detractors say that the action was premature. In their view, the technology has not developed sufficiently; a standard that seems appropriate may later turn out to be short-sighted or even wrong-minded. Yet at the same time, several corporations, including AT&T, have begun offering equipment that adheres to ISDN standards of their own, with the hope that their specifications will win out.

Initial confusion aside, the idea of an ISDN is so compelling that most telecommunications experts believe a universal network is inevitable. It is the logical extension of a decades-long process in telecommunications. Computers have made telecommunications increasingly digital, which in turn has extended the influence of computers into every corner of society. As the process continues, the line between computing and communicating will become increasingly blurred. In the age of information, the combination matters more than the individual ingredients.

A Seven-Layer Blueprint for Communications

3

The problem of getting a computer of one brand to accept data created by another manufacturer's machine has confronted users of these devices since their earliest days. At one time the only practical way around this barrier was to retype the data from one computer into the second — a time-consuming procedure fraught with the potential for error.

As computers proliferated, interfaces, or adapters, were invented that translated one machine's code into a form that others could understand, allowing a variety of computers to be hooked together in networks. But these interfaces were expensive, both in the aggregate, because a substantial number of them were needed to establish a large network, and singly, because each type of computer needed an interface of its own. Consequently, there was little opportunity to spread the cost of developing a given interface by selling many copies of it.

Networking would be facilitated and the expense much reduced if computer builders could agree on how to construct their products, so that each could communicate with the others. Toward this end, in 1977, the Geneva-based International Organization for Standardization set forth the Open Systems Interconnection (OSI) model.

A master plan for computer-to-computer dialogue, the OSI model divides the communications process into seven layers, which are described on the following pages. Like a good building code, the model sets standards that permit a wide variety in the design of computer hardware and software. The model demands only that communications tasks remain in their assigned layers and that the output of each layer precisely matches the format established for it. Employing software created with the model's requirements in mind, users of computers built to conform to the plan are able to send data to and from one another's machines almost effortlessly.

05

The Structure of the OSI Model

This illustration, dissected and explained in detail on the following pages, outlines how the OSI seven-layer model speeds computer data from a terminal of one host computer, through a network and ultimately to a terminal of another host computer.

Before data can be transmitted, each OSI layer in the send-ing host computer *(below)* establishes with the corresponding layer in the receiving host *(right)* the applicable ground rules for a communications session: type of transmission, computer alphabet to be used, error-checking method and the like. This procedure, called peer-to-peer communication, is represent-ed here as colored bands between host-computer layers; in actuality, the dialogue occurs over the same path that data takes through the OSI model and the network.

Data to be communicated, represented by a white ribbon, originates at the sending host computer and passes through each OSI layer on its way to the network. As the informa-tion descends through each layer, it undergoes a transfor-

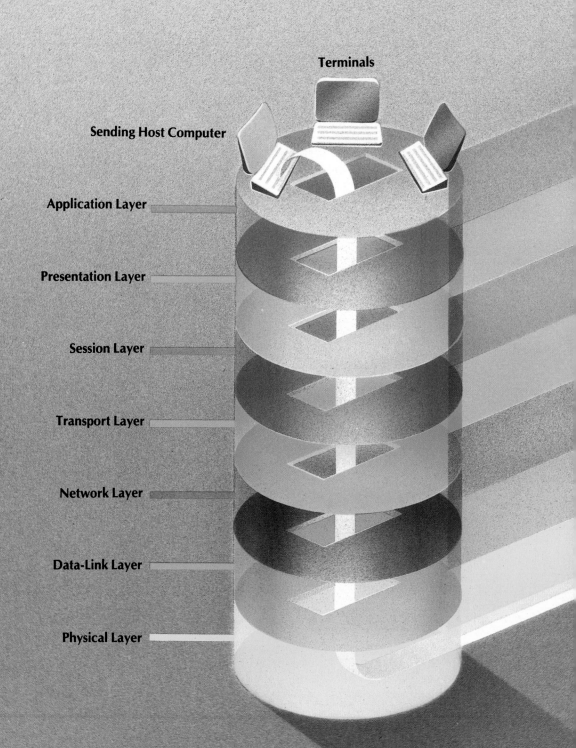

Terminals

Sending Host Computer

Application Layer

Presentation Layer

Session Layer

Transport Layer

Network Layer

Data-Link Layer

Physical Layer

mation that prepares it for processing by the next layer.

Upon reaching the bottom layer, data is passed to the network as a serial stream of bits represented by changing voltages, microwaves or light pulses. In this example, the information is relayed to the receiving host by a single network node, or switching center (*pages 66-67*); in practice, data passes through many nodes, some of which may be host computers. Each node examines the data to determine its destination, then reprocesses it and sends it on.

At the receiving host, the stream of bits travels in reverse order through the seven OSI layers. The data is then displayed on a terminal in its original form.

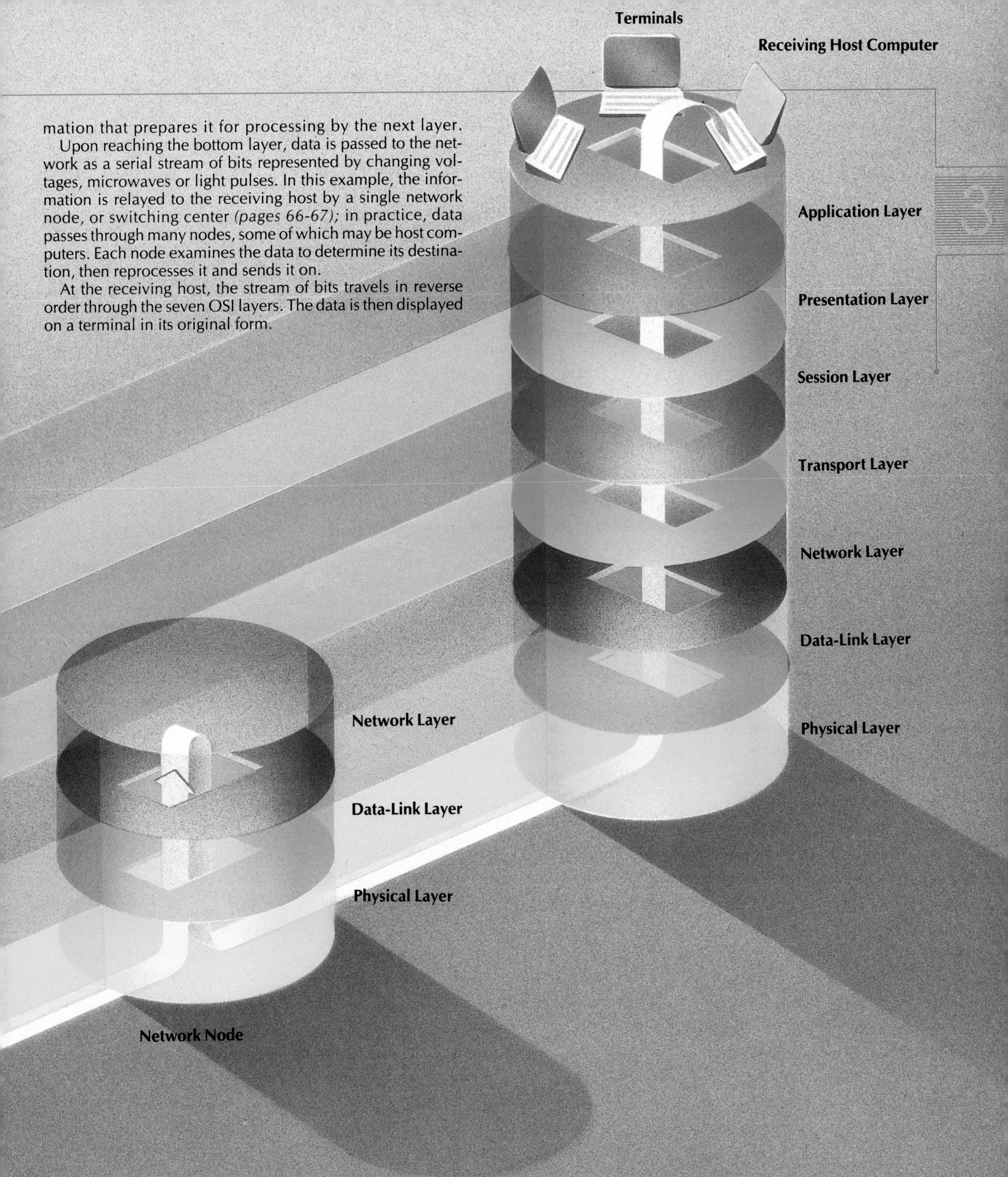

Terminals

Receiving Host Computer

Application Layer

Presentation Layer

Session Layer

Transport Layer

Network Layer

Data-Link Layer

Physical Layer

Network Layer

Data-Link Layer

Physical Layer

Network Node

Starting a Message through the System

A message transmitted between two computers in a network begins the journey in the application and presentation layers at the top of the OSI model. In these layers are determined the type of message to be sent — numerical data, text or instructions to a program that resides in a distant host — and the form that the message will take.

The application layer (blue) is the only part of the OSI model that a computer user sees, as it fills requests to work with various application programs — word-processing software, perhaps — and with information such as a shared data base that may be found either in the local host or in one elsewhere on the network. Behind the scenes, this layer takes the first steps in preparing a message, shown as a white ribbon, for transmission.

Following the activities of the application layer, the presentation layer (pink) ensures that the message takes a form the receiving host can interpret. Three of the several functions that can occur in this layer are detailed below.

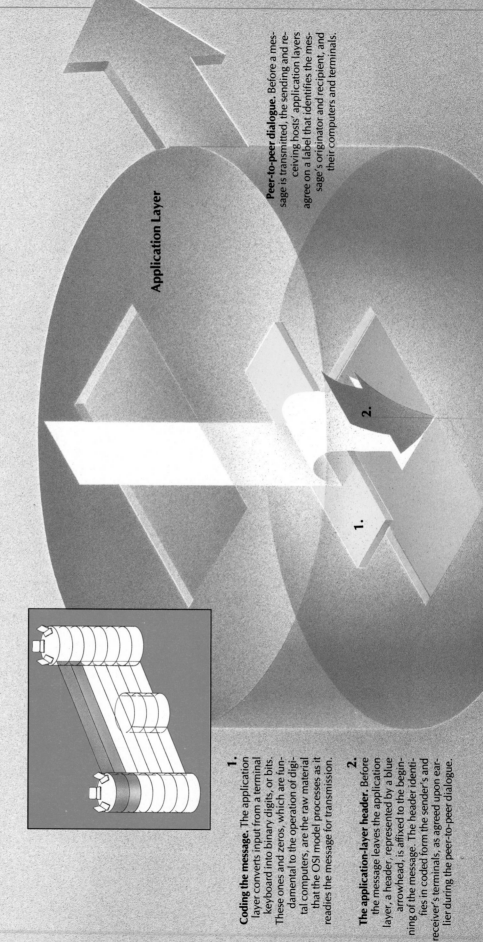

Application Layer

Peer-to-peer dialogue. Before a message is transmitted, the sending and receiving hosts' application layers agree on a label that identifies the message's originator and recipient, and their computers and terminals.

1.

2.

1. Coding the message. The application layer converts input from a terminal keyboard into binary digits, or bits. These ones and zeros, which are fundamental to the operation of digital computers, are the raw material that the OSI model processes as it readies the message for transmission.

2. The application-layer header. Before the message leaves the application layer, a header, represented by a blue arrowhead, is affixed to the beginning of the message. The header identifies in coded form the sender's and receiver's terminals, as agreed upon earlier during the peer-to-peer dialogue.

Peer-to-peer dialogue. The sending host's presentation layer confers with its peer at the receiving end to agree on a computer alphabet — usually ASCII — for the eventual transmission of a message. Schemes for compressing data (4) and encrypting it (5) may also be established at this level.

Presentation Layer

3.
Using a common language. If the hosts use different alphabets, the message, upon entering the sending computer's presentation layer, is translated — typically from the originator's alphabet into that of the recipient.

4.
Shrinking the data. The presentation layer may compress data to reduce transmission and storage costs. Compression shortens a message by employing codes as stand-ins for often-repeated terms, such as "credit" or "debit" in an accounting system.

5.
Ensuring privacy. To keep information confidential, data may be encrypted in the sending host's presentation layer according to rules agreed on earlier, during the peer-to-peer dialogue.

6.
The presentation-layer header. A header, coded with the alphabet to be used as well as details of any compression or encryption schemes that apply, is attached to the message as it passes to the session layer (overleaf).

Establishing a Connection

The next two layers in the OSI model manage the communications between hosts. On instructions from the user issued through the application layer, the session layer (*purple*) opens communications with a distant host. This layer also determines whether the two hosts will be able to address each other simultaneously (*full duplex*) or must take turns (*half duplex*). After all messages have been transmitted and replies

received, the session layer concludes communications by signing off from the network.

The primary responsibility of the transport layer (*green*) is to ensure that a message arrives at the correct destination in exactly the same form as it was sent. In doing so, it monitors acknowledgments from the receiving host that messages have arrived safely.

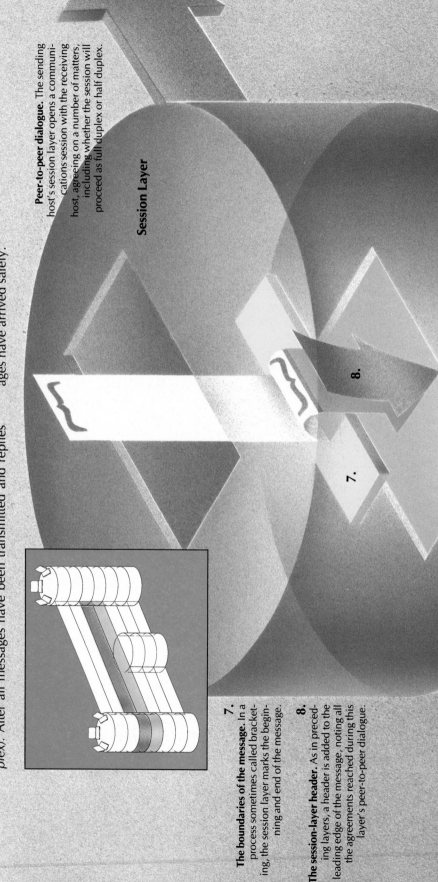

Session Layer

Peer-to-peer dialogue. The sending host's session layer opens a communications session with the receiving host, agreeing on a number of matters, including whether the session will proceed as full duplex or half duplex.

7.

8.

7. **The boundaries of the message.** In a process sometimes called bracketing, the session layer marks the beginning and end of the message.

8. **The session-layer header.** As in preceding layers, a header is added to the leading edge of the message, noting all the agreements reached during this layer's peer-to-peer dialogue.

Transport Layer

Peer-to-peer dialogue. Before communication can begin, the transport layers of the OSI model must agree on a convention for assigning job and process codes to messages. These codes translate the label attached to the message by the application layer into symbols that the transport layers can interpret.

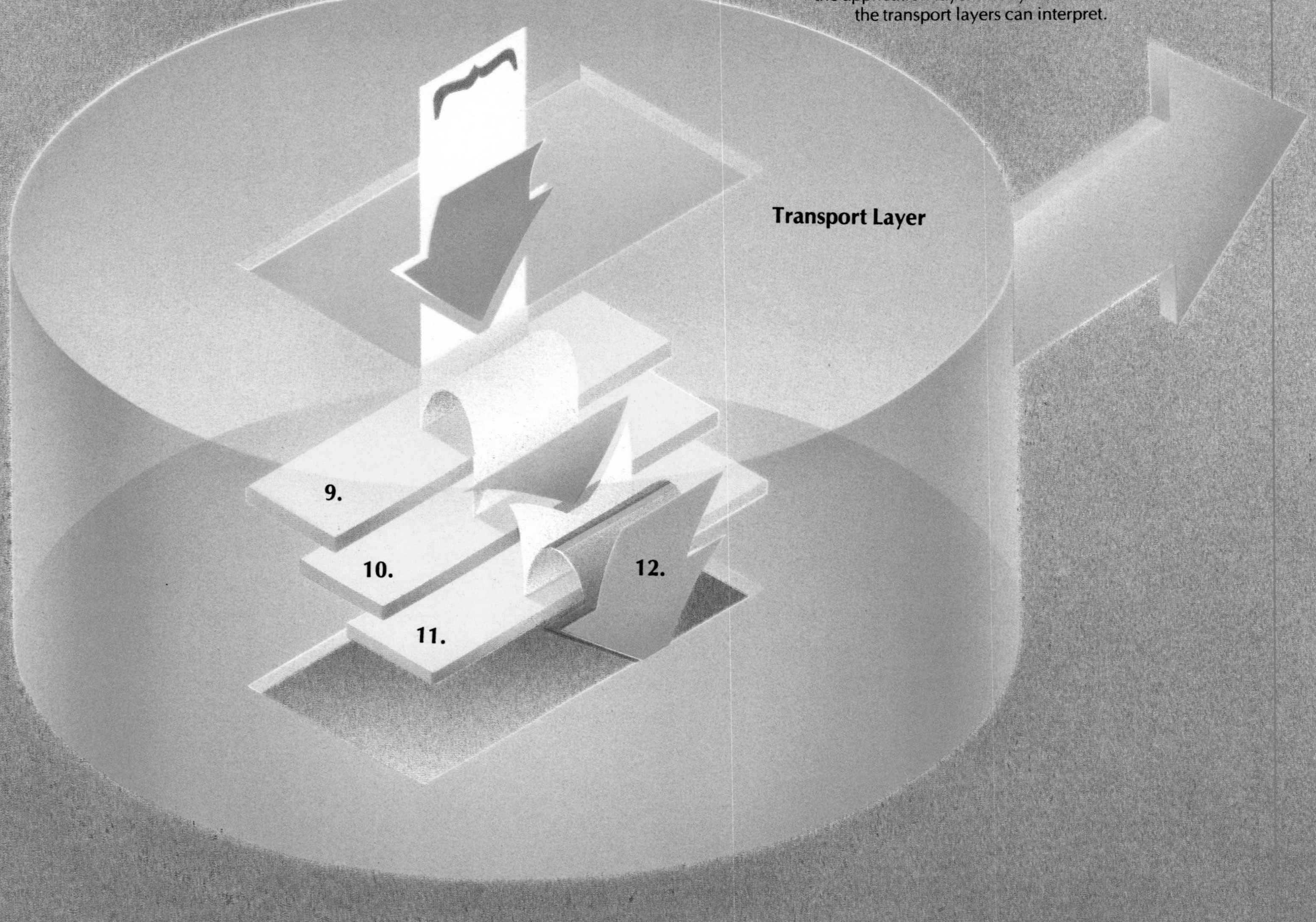

9.
Subdividing the message. The transport layer breaks the message into segments, keeping track of their sequence in the message. Each segment is assigned a checksum, a value derived from the bits in the segment. The receiving host uses the checksum to ascertain whether the bits have been rearranged or lost in transit.

10.
Duplicating the segments. After dividing the message into segments, the transport layer makes a backup copy of each one; the copy can be transmitted should the original be damaged or destroyed en route.

11.
Erasing backup copies. When the transport layer in the sending host receives acknowledgment from the receiver that a unit has arrived intact, the backup copy is discarded.

12.
The transport-layer header. To each segment of the message is affixed a new header that contains the segment's checksum and its position in the message. The lead segment also carries the headers applied in the preceding three layers of the OSI process.

111

Routes, Packets and Bits in the Subnet

The bottom three layers of the OSI model, known as the subnet, have the job of routing messages through the network. Each subnet layer plays a different management role. The network layer (brown) selects a route for the message. Once the sequence of nodes is determined, the data-link layer (orange) assigns messages to specific communications channels and temporarily stores data in memory if the volume of infor-

mation threatens to overwhelm the channel as it passes to the network through the physical layer (yellow).

At this level of the OSI model, peer-to-peer communications between the two hosts no longer occur. Instead, every computer taking part in the transmission, whether a host or a network node, relays information to the next computer along the route to the receiving host.

Peer-to-peer dialogue. The network layers of the sending host and the nodes en route to the receiving host initiate, maintain and terminate the connection for each leg of the journey.

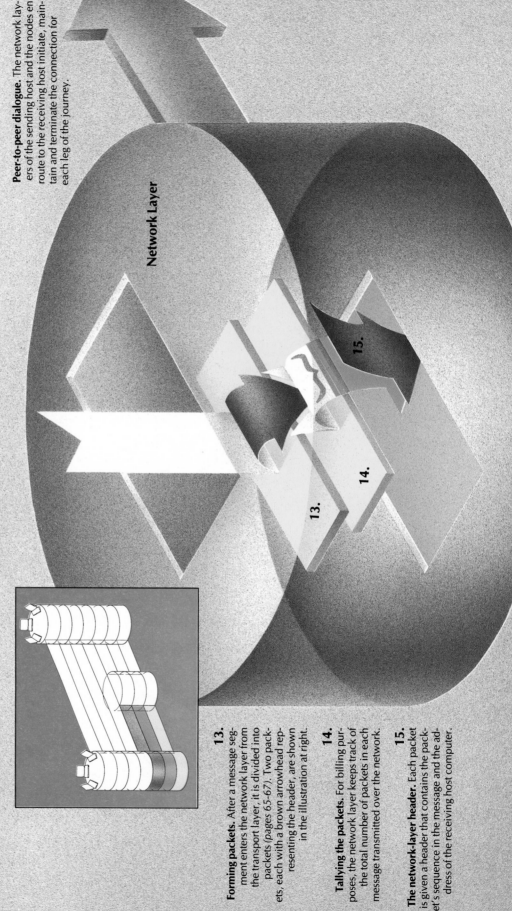

Network Layer

13.
Forming packets. After a message segment enters the network layer from the transport layer, it is divided into packets (pages 65-67). Two packets, each with a brown arrowhead representing the header, are shown in the illustration at right.

14.
Tallying the packets. For billing purposes, the network layer keeps track of the total number of packets in each message transmitted over the network.

15.
The network-layer header. Each packet is given a header that contains the packet's sequence in the message and the address of the receiving host computer.

Data-Link Layer

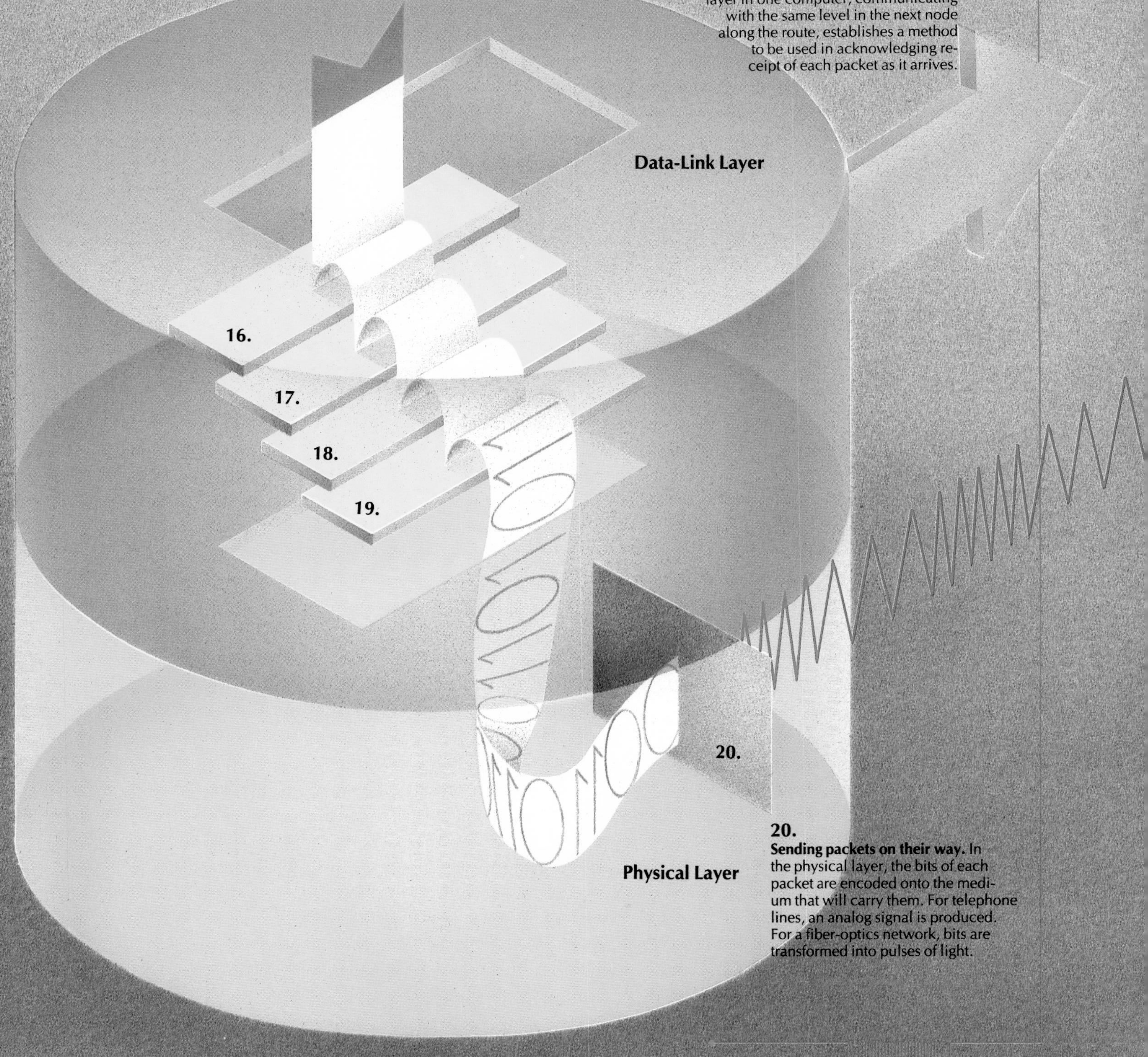

Peer-to-peer dialogue. The data-link layer in one computer, communicating with the same level in the next node along the route, establishes a method to be used in acknowledging receipt of each packet as it arrives.

Physical Layer

20.
Sending packets on their way. In the physical layer, the bits of each packet are encoded onto the medium that will carry them. For telephone lines, an analog signal is produced. For a fiber-optics network, bits are transformed into pulses of light.

16.
A checksum for the subnet. In the data-link layer, a checksum is calculated for each message packet. This checksum is used to confirm that a packet has completed each stage of the journey intact.

17.
Addressing the packets. The network address of the next stop each packet will make on the way to the receiving host is added to the packet.

18.
Framing the packets. The data-link layer marks the end of each packet, as shown in orange in the drawing at right. A header at the front of each packet, illustrated as ones and zeros descending into the next layer, contains the node's address and checksum. Together the header and the end marker constitute the packet's frame, or boundaries.

19.
Duplicating the packets. The data-link layer makes and holds a copy of every packet until it receives acknowledgment from the next point along the route that the packet has arrived undamaged. The copy is then discarded.

113

Relay through an Intermediate Node

The role of node in a network may be played either by a host computer or, as shown here, by a specialized processor dedicated to the job. Each node contains the OSI model's three subnet layers, the minimum requirement for the work of assessing whether a packet has arrived intact, determining the next leg of its journey and sending it on its way.

Beginning with Step 21 (bottom), the drawings below follow a packet up through the node, then out again as it zips toward the next stop. When a packet arrives at a node, operations performed earlier by the sending host's subnet are unraveled: Headers are read, checksums tallied and acknowledgments returned to the sending host informing it that the packet has arrived undamaged.

At the top of the subnet, the network layer selects the route for the next hop toward the receiving host. As the packet moves back down the node, the subnet reinserts checksums and headers, then makes a copy before sending the packet to its next stop.

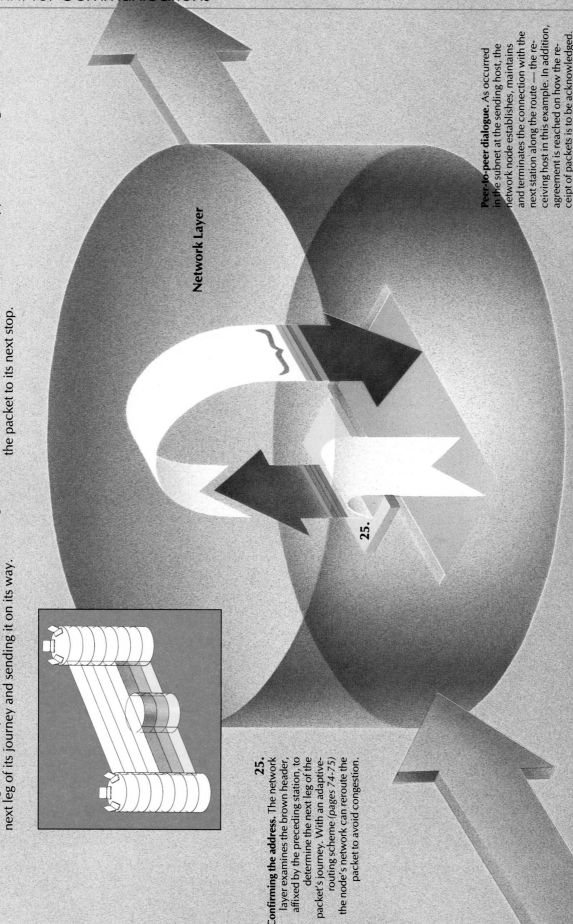

Network Layer

25.

Confirming the address. The network layer examines the brown header, affixed by the preceding station, to determine the next leg of the packet's journey. With an adaptive-routing scheme (pages 74-75) the node's network can reroute the packet to avoid congestion.

Peer-to-peer dialogue. As occurred in the subnet at the sending host, the network node establishes, maintains and terminates the connection with the next station along the route — the receiving host in this example. In addition, agreement is reached on how the receipt of packets is to be acknowledged.

26.
Reinserting the checksum. The data-link layer once again recalculates the checksum for each packet.

Data-Link Layer

27.
Addressing the packets. Each packet now receives the address for the next point in the journey.

28.
Framing the packets. The data-link layer reframes each packet with a header at the beginning and a marker at the end.

29.
Duplicating the packets. Before a packet passes to the physical layer, a copy is made of it. The duplicate is held until confirmation is received that the packet has arrived safely at the next stop.

Physical Layer

30.
Sending packets on their way. The physical layer reencodes the bits of each packet into the proper form for transmission and sends them on.

24.
Unframing the packets. The header and end marker are stripped from each packet as it moves to the network layer.

23.
Checking for errors. If the two checksums match, no error has occurred in transmission and the node acknowledges receipt of the packet, referring to it by number. Checksums that differ prompt a request that the packet be retransmitted.

22.
Logging-in the packets. Noting the sequence number in the header of each packet, the data-link layer recalculates its checksum and compares it with the checksum in the header.

21.
Arriving at a node. Carried by wires or other media, the signal containing a message enters a network node by way of the physical layer. There, the signal is decoded and retranslated into bits.

115

Gateway to the Receiving Host

In many networking systems, host computers are equipped to play the role of a node: When such a computer is functioning as a receiving host, it forwards — by the procedures explained on the preceding two pages — packets that are just passing through and traps packets addressed to it.

Packets that a host keeps undergo inspection and restoration as they progress upward through the OSI model, beginning with the physical layer at the bottom of the page.

The operations performed by the receiving host consist mainly of inspecting control data encoded in the headers attached by each layer in the sending host. The headers are then stripped away and discarded as the packets are reassembled step by step into the message originally transmitted by the sending host.

38.
Detaching the header. As they progress to the transport layer, packets are stripped of the header that contains the packet number and the address of the receiving host.

37.
Tallying the packets. For billing purposes — and as a cross-check on the sending host — the network layer re-counts incoming packets.

Network Layer

36.
Recreating message segments. The network layer reassembles the packets into message segments using the sequence number in each header to arrange the packets in order.

35.
Sorting by destination. The network layer checks the address of each packet. Those destined for a different host are readdressed and sent on their way. Packets bearing the address of the receiving host pass to the transport layer.

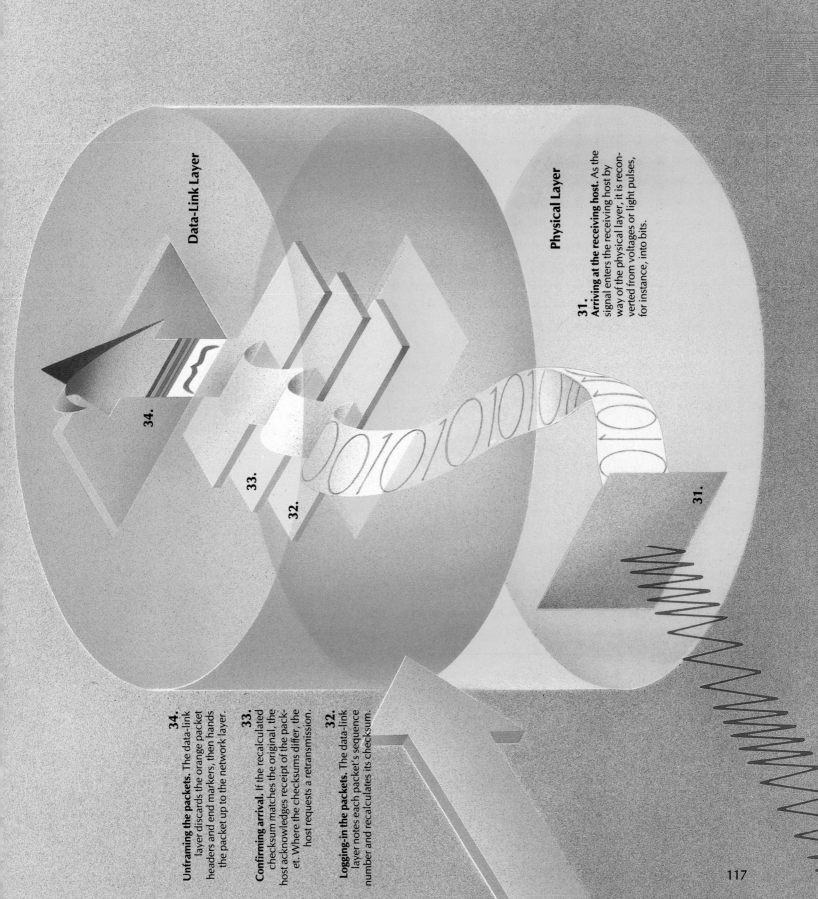

Data-Link Layer

34.
Unframing the packets. The data-link layer discards the orange packet headers and end markers, then hands the packet up to the network layer.

33.
Confirming arrival. If the recalculated checksum matches the original, the host acknowledges receipt of the packet. Where the checksums differ, the host requests a retransmission.

32.
Logging-in the packets. The data-link layer notes each packet's sequence number and recalculates its checksum.

Physical Layer

31.
Arriving at the receiving host. As the signal enters the receiving host by way of the physical layer, it is reconverted from voltages or light pulses, for instance, into bits.

117

From Many Packets, a Single Message

Together, the transport layer and the session layer in the receiving host reconstruct the original message from the segments handed up by the network layer. In addition to its part in assembling the message, the transport layer (bottom) converts the job and process numbers assigned by its peer at the sending host (page 111) into a form that will be recognizable by the receiving host's application layer. The session layer, as a safeguard against passing on incomplete information, holds the message until the data is complete. Only then does the session layer pass the message to the layers above, where partial information might ruin a data base or financial analysis.

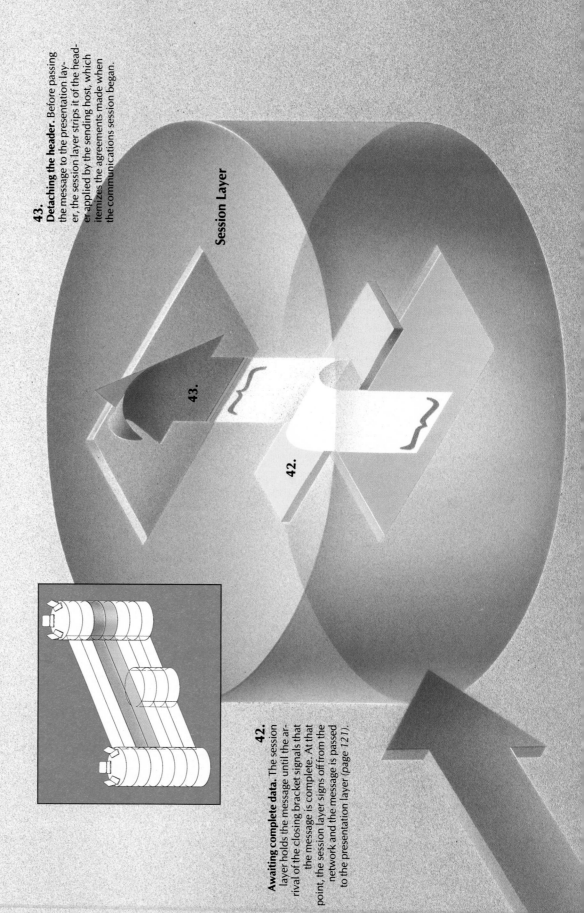

Session Layer

43.
Detaching the header. Before passing the message to the presentation layer, the session layer strips it of the header applied by the sending host, which itemizes the agreements made when the communications session began.

42.
Awaiting complete data. The session layer holds the message until the arrival of the closing bracket signals that the message is complete. At that point, the session layer signs off from the network and the message is passed to the presentation layer (page 121).

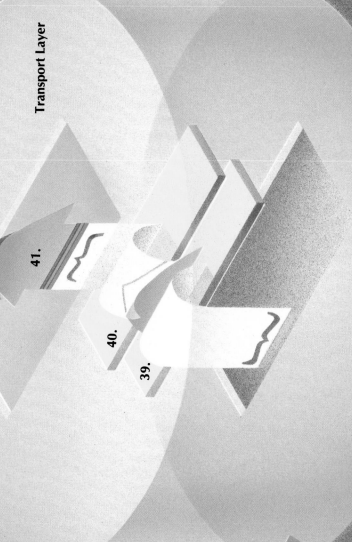

Transport Layer

41.
Detaching the header. Before a segment of the message enters the session layer, the transport layer strips away the header that contains the unit's checksum and a sequence number, and discards it.

40.
Confirming the contents. The transport layer recalculates the checksum for each message segment and compares it with the original. If they match, verification of a successful transmission is passed to the sending host. Otherwise, the transport layer asks its peer in the sending host to retransmit the message segment.

39.
Reassembling the message. The transport layer strings together, according to sequence numbers in the header, message segments that have been passed on by the network layer.

Preparation for Journey's End

Nearing its destination—a terminal connected to the receiving host computer—the message arrives at the presentation and application layers. As in the sending host (*pages 108-109*), the presentation layer at this end has few network-management responsibilities. Rather, it is concerned chiefly with the form in which the message was transmitted: alphabet, compression and encryption.

The application layer, which controls the use of software accessible through the network, such as word-processing or data-base programs, displays the message on the appropriate terminal in a format compatible with the receiving system.

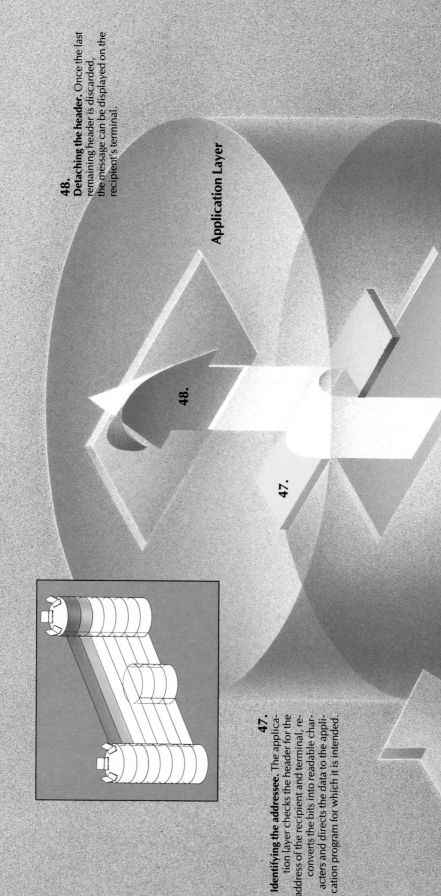

48.
Detaching the header. Once the last remaining header is discarded, the message can be displayed on the recipient's terminal.

Application Layer

48.

47.

47.
Identifying the addressee. The application layer checks the header for the address of the recipient and terminal, reconverts the bits into readable characters and directs the data to the application program for which it is intended.

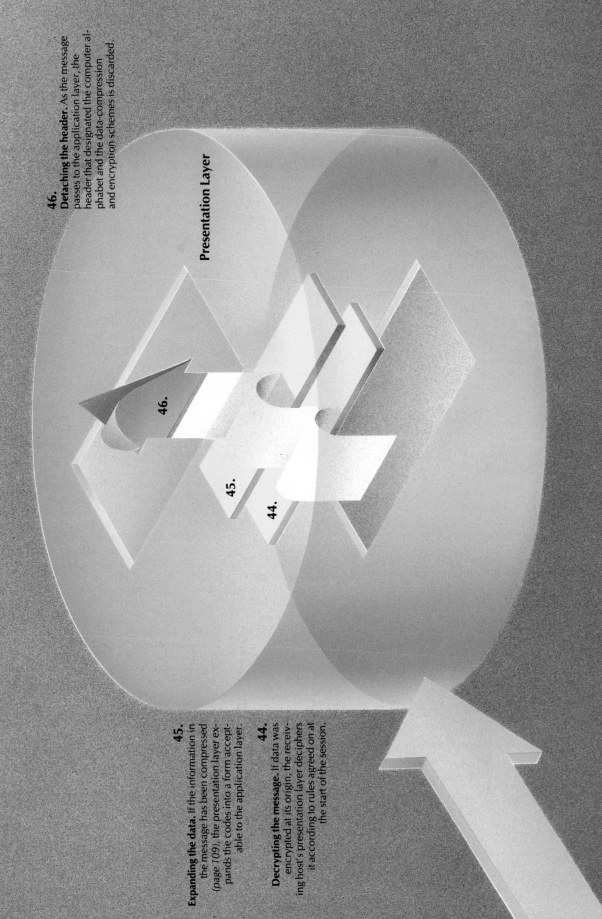

46.

Detaching the header. As the message passes to the application layer, the header that designated the computer alphabet and the data-compression and encryption schemes is discarded.

Presentation Layer

46.

45.

44.

45.

Expanding the data. If the information in the message has been compressed (page 109), the presentation layer expands the codes into a form acceptable to the application layer.

44.

Decrypting the message. If data was encrypted at its origin, the receiving host's presentation layer deciphers it according to rules agreed on at the start of the session.

Glossary

Acoustic coupler: a type of telecommunications equipment that permits the transmission of computer data over the telephone network through the handset of a telephone.

Adaptive equalizer: electronic equipment designed to maximize the rate at which computer data may be transmitted over long-distance telephone lines; while a call is in progress, the equalizer continually compensates for distortion in the connection.

Amplitude: in communications, the height of a wave and a measure of its strength; the amplitude of a sound wave, for example, is a measure of the loudness of the sound.

Amplitude-shift keying: a technique for representing the binary digits zero and one by varying the amplitude of a wave-shaped signal between two designated levels.

Analog: the representation of a continuously changing physical variable (sound, for example) by another physical variable (such as electrical current).

ASCII: the acronym for American Standard Code for Information Interchange, a widely used system for encoding letters, numerals, punctuation marks and signs as seven-place binary numbers.

Automatic equalizer: *see* Adaptive equalizer.

Bandwidth: the range of frequencies occupied by an information-bearing signal or that can be accommodated by a transmission medium such as copper wires, microwaves or optical fibers. The greater the bandwidth, the more data can be transmitted.

Baud: one change in the amplitude, phase or frequency of a signal, used to encode the signal with digital information.

Binary: having two components or possible states; usually represented by a code of zeros and ones.

Bit: the smallest unit of information in a binary computer, represented by a single zero or one. The word "bit" is a contraction of "binary digit."

Buffer: a space reserved in a computer's memory for temporarily storing data, often just before it is to be transmitted or after it has been received.

Bus topology: a layout for a local area network in which network stations are linked by means of an open-ended cable or other transmission medium.

Carrier: a signal whose amplitude, phase or frequency is altered by another, information-bearing signal in order to convey the information.

Carrier-sense multiple access (CSMA): a method for determining when a station may send data over a local area network; before transmitting, the station confirms that the network is idle by noting the absence of the carrier signal.

Checksum: a number derived from the sequence of ones and zeros in a stream of data and used to detect transmission errors.

Circuit switching: a method of networking in which communicating machines have exclusive use of the circuit linking them — even during pauses, when the circuit is momentarily idle — until the circuit is released.

Coaxial cable: a transmission medium composed of an insulated copper wire inside a tubular conductor.

Codec: the abbreviation for coder/decoder, a device used in digital telephone systems to convert analog signals to digital ones and vice versa; *see* Modem.

Collision detection: a refinement of carrier-sense multiple access (CSMA) that allows a station to detect and compensate for the scrambling of data that occurs on the network when stations begin transmitting simultaneously.

Common carrier: a company selling communications or transportation services to the public.

Datagram: a packet-switching method in which messages are divided into self-contained data packets that can be routed through the network independently and reassembled at their destination into the original message.

Digital: pertaining to the representation, manipulation or transmission of information by discrete, or on-off, signals.

Digitize: to represent data in digital, or discrete, form or to convert an analog, or continuous, signal to such a form.

Earth station: a communications installation capable of transmitting, receiving and processing data relayed by satellite.

EBCDIC: the acronym for Extended Binary Coded Decimal Interchange Code, an IBM system for encoding letters, numerals, punctuation marks and signs that accommodates twice as many symbols and functions as ASCII by using eight-place binary numbers instead of seven-place numbers.

Echo: a reverberation caused by the tendency of different frequencies in a signal to travel over a wire at slightly different speeds.

Electromagnetic waves: a form of radiant energy, such as light and radio waves, produced as a result of interacting electric and magnetic fields.

Fiber optics: the technology of encoding data as pulses of light beamed through ultrathin strands of glass.

Frequency: the number of times per second that a wave cycle (one peak and one trough) repeats.

Frequency-division multiplexing: a technique used to transmit multiple communications simultaneously over a single circuit by dividing the transmission path's bandwidth into several narrower bands, each carrying a single communication.

Frequency-shift keying: a method of impressing binary data on a carrier signal by switching the carrier between two frequencies, one signifying zeros and the other representing ones.

Full duplex: describing a communications system that makes possible the simultaneous transmission of information by two participants engaged in an exchange of data.

Geostationary: pertaining to an orbit 22,300 miles above the equator where, to an observer on earth, a satellite appears to be stationary.

Gigahertz (GHZ): one billion hertz.

Half duplex: describing a communications system in which the partners in an exchange of data must take turns transmitting.

Handshake: the exchange of control information that takes place between computerized communications devices before data can be transferred between them.

Hertz: a unit of frequency equal to one cycle per second.

Intelligent modem: one that facilitates communication by performing some functions automatically — hanging up on a busy signal, for example — and that accepts instructions from a computer keyboard for such tasks as dialing a telephone number or breaking a connection.

Interface message processor (IMP): a computer that connects other computers to a network.

Local area network (LAN): a system of computer hardware and software that links computers, printers and other peripherals into a network suitable for transmission of data between offices in a building, for example, or between buildings situated near one another.

Logic gate: a circuit that accepts one or more inputs and always produces a single, predictable output.

Megahertz (MHZ): one million hertz.

Microwave: any electromagnetic wave in the radio frequency spectrum above one gigahertz.

Microwave link: a communications path over which information is conveyed by microwave transmissions.

Modem: the abbreviation for modulator/demodulator, a device that is used with analog telephone systems to convert digital signals to analog ones and analog signals to digital; *see* Codec.

Modulation: the process of encoding one signal with information contained in another signal.

Multimode optical fiber: an optical fiber with a relatively large center, or core, that allows light pulses to take many paths and lose definition, reducing the number of bits per second the fiber can transmit accurately over distance.

Multiplexing: a technique that allows multiple transmissions of information or data to share a single communications link.

Node: a junction of communications paths in a network.

Open Systems Interconnections (OSI): standardized communications procedures that make possible the linking of diverse data-processing systems by means of networks.

Optical fiber: a fine thread of glass that carries light pulses in optical communications systems.

Packet: a segment of a digitized message that is transmitted through a network independent of other segments from the same message.

Packet switching: the process of dividing a digitized message into packets and transmitting them independently to their destination on a network, where they are reassembled.

Phase modulation: the process of shifting from one point, or phase, in a wave cycle to another to encode digital information on a carrier of a given frequency.

Pitch: the highness or lowness of sound.

Protocol: a set of strict rules governing the internal workings of a communications system.

Pulse code modulation: a digitizing process in which an analog, or continuous, signal is represented in digital, or discrete, form.

Repeater: equipment that forwards an electronic signal over a network, usually after amplifying an analog signal or after regenerating the bits in a digital one.

Ring topology: a layout for a local area network in which network stations are connected to one another by a closed loop of cable or other transmission medium.

RS-232: a mechanical and electrical standard that permits the trans-

fer of information between computers and communications equipment, and is also used to connect terminals, printers and other peripheral devices.

Single-mode fiber: a type of optical fiber that restricts light to one mode, or path, along the center of the fiber, maximizing its information-carrying capacity.

Station: any computer, printer, data-storage device or other computer peripheral connected to a local area network.

Telegraphy: a low-speed form of digital communications in which letters and numerals are transmitted by coded pulses of electricity.

Teletypewriter: telegraphy apparatus that transmits coded pulses of electricity from a typewriter-like keyboard.

Terminal interface processor (TIP): a computer that connects terminals directly to a network, eliminating the need for a host computer.

Time-division multiplexing: a transmission technique for digital information in which a communications channel is divided into time slots, allowing data from multiple sources to be interleaved and sent concurrently over a single communications link.

Time sharing: the simultaneous use of a computer by more than one person.

Token access: a means of transmitting data over a local area network that employs a circulating token — actually, a special sequence of bits — to which a station attaches its data.

Twisted-pair wire: a transmission medium consisting of two insulated copper wires twisted around each other; traditionally used in the telephone system.

Value-added network (VAN): a data network that supplements basic communications services acquired from a common carrier with additional features that correct transmission errors and ensure compatibility between dissimilar computers and terminals.

Waveguide: a metal tube used to transmit microwaves.

X.25: an international standard for connecting computers or terminals to a network that operates by means of packet switching.

X.75: an international standard which provides for interconnections between data networks of different nations.

Bibliography

Books

Augarten, Stan, *Bit by Bit*. New York: Ticknor & Fields, 1984.

Bennet, William R., and James R. Davey, *Data Transmission*. New York: McGraw-Hill Book Co., 1965.

Bernstein, Jeremey, *Three Degrees below Zero*. New York: Charles Scribner's Sons, 1984.

Black, Harold S., *Modulation Theory*. New York: D. Van Nostrand Reinhold Co., 1960.

Bleazard, G. B., *Introducing Satellite Communications*. Manchester, England: The National Computing Centre Limited, 1985.

Bleiler, E. F., ed., *Science Fiction Writers*. New York: Charles Scribner's Sons, 1982.

Brock, Gerald W., *The Telecommunications Industry — The Dynamics of Market Structure*. Cambridge, Mass.: Harvard University Press, 1981.

Brooks, John, *Telephone: The First Hundred Years*. New York: Harper & Row, 1975.

Ceruzzi, Paul E., *Reckoners: The Prehistory of the Digital Computer, from Relays to the Stored Program Concept*. Westport, Conn.: Greenwood Press, 1983.

Chou, Wushow, ed., *Computer Communications:*
Vol. 1, *Principles*. Englewood Cliffs, N.J.: Prentice-Hall, 1983.

Vol. 2, *Systems and Applications*. Englewood Cliffs, N.J.: Prentice-Hall, 1985.

Datapro Management of Data Communications. Vols. 1 and 2. Delran N.J.: Datapro Research Corp., February 1986.

Datapro Reports on Data Communications. Vols. 1, 2 and 3. Delran, N.J.: Datapro Research Corp., February 1986.

Deasington, R. J., *X.25 Explained: Protocols for Packet Switching Networks*. West Sussex, England: Ellis Horwood Limited, 1985.

Dunlap, Orrin E.:
Communications in Space: From Marconi to Man on the Moon. New York: Harper & Row 1962.

Communications in Space: From Wireless to Satellite Relay. New York: Harper & Row, 1964.

Fagen, M. D., ed., *A History of Engineering and Science in the Bell System: National Service in War and Peace (1925-1975)*. Murray Hill, N.J.: Bell Telephone Laboratories, 1978.

Fike, John L., and George E. Friend, *Understanding Telephone Electronics*. Fort Worth: Texas Instruments Learning Center, 1983.

Gatland, Kenneth William, ed., *Telecommunications Satellites*. Englewood Cliffs, N.J.: Prentice-Hall, 1964.

Green, Paul E., Jr., ed., *Computer Communications*. New York: IEEE Press, 1974.

Harlow, Alvin F., *Old Wires and New Waves.* New York: Arno Press, 1971 (reprint of 1936 edition).

House, William C., ed., *Electronic Communications Systems.* New York: Petrocelli Books, 1980.

Jaffe, Leonard, *Communications in Space.* New York: Holt, Rinehart and Winston, 1966.

Johnson, Brian, *The Secret War.* London: BBC, 1978.

Kapany, N. S., and J. J. Burke, *Optical Waveguides.* New York: Academic Press, 1972.

Keiser, Bernhard E., and Eugene Strange, *Digital Telephony and Network Integration.* New York: Van Nostrand Reinhold Co., 1985.

Laver, Murray, *Computers, Communications and Society.* London: Oxford University Press, 1975.

Leinwoll, Stanley:
From Spark to Satellite. New York: Charles Scribner's Sons, 1979.
Space Communications. New York: John F. Rider, 1964.

Loomis, Mary E. S., *Data Communications.* Englewood Cliffs, N.J.: Prentice-Hall, 1983.

Luecke, Gerald, and Charles W. Battle, eds., *Radio Shack, Understanding Data Communications.* Ft. Worth: Texas Instruments Information Publishing Center, 1984.

Lukashok, Alvin, *Communication Satellites: How They Work.* New York: G. P. Putnam's Sons, 1967.

Lustig, Lawrence K., ed., *Impact.* Murray Hill, N.J.: Bell Laboratories, 1981.

Mabon, Prescott C., *Mission Communications: The Story of Bell Laboratories.* Murray Hill, N.J.: Bell Telephone Laboratories, 1975.

The McGraw-Hill Encyclopedia of Space. New York: McGraw-Hill Book Co., 1968.

The McGraw-Hill Yearbook of Science and Technology. New York: McGraw-Hill Book Co., 1982.

Martin, James:
Future Developments in Telecommunication. Englewood Cliffs, N.J.: Prentice-Hall, 1977.
Telecommunications and the Computer. Englewood Cliffs, N.J.: Prentice-Hall, 1976.

Mathison, Stuart L., and Philip M. Walker, *Computers and Telecommunications: Issues in Public Policy.* Englewood Cliffs, N.J.: Prentice-Hall, 1970.

Miller, Stuart E., and Alan G. Chynoweth, eds., *Optical Fiber Telecommunications.* New York: Academic Press, 1979.

Millman, S., ed., *A History of Engineering and Science in the Bell System: Communications Sciences, 1925-1980.* Murray Hill, N.J.: AT&T Bell Laboratories, 1984.

O'Neill, E. F., ed., *A History of Engineering and Science in the Bell System — Transmission Technology, 1925-1975.* Murray Hill, N.J.: AT&T Bell Laboratories, 1985.

Pierce, John R.:
The Beginnings of Satellite Communications. San Francisco: San Francisco Press, 1968.
SIGNALS: The Telephone and Beyond. San Francisco: W. H. Freeman and Co., 1981.

Pouzin, Louis, and Hubert Zimmermann, *Advances in Computer Communications and Networking.* Dedham, Mass.: Artech House, 1979.

Prentiss, Stan, *Satellite Communications.* Blue Ridge Summit, Pa.: Tab Books, 1983.

Ralston, Anthony, ed., *Encyclopedia of Computer Science and Engineering.* New York: Van Nostrand Reinhold Co., 1983.

Rey, R. F., ed., *Engineering and Operations in the Bell System.* Murray Hill, N.J.: AT&T Bell Laboratories, 1983.

Rosner, Roy D., *Packet Switching, Tomorrow's Communications Today.* Belmont, Calif.: Wadsworth, 1982.

Scott, P.R.D., *Modems in Data Communications.* Manchester, England: The National Computing Center, 1980.

Seyer, Martin D., *RS-232 Made Easy, Connecting Computers, Printers, Terminals, and Modems.* Englewood Cliffs, N.J.: Prentice-Hall, 1984.

Stallings, William:
Data and Computer Communications. New York: Macmillan Publishing Co., 1985.
Local Networks: An Introduction. New York: Macmillan Publishing Co., 1984.

Tanenbaum, Andrew S., *Computer Networks.* Englewood Cliffs, N.J.: Prentice-Hall, 1981.

Wymer, Norman, *From Marconi to Telstar.* London: Longmans, 1966.

Periodicals

Andrews, E. G., "Telephone Switching and the Early Bell Laboratories Computers." *The Bell System Technical Journal,* March 1963.

Ash, Gerald R., and Vernon S. Mummert, "AT&T Carves New Routes in Its Nationwide Network." *AT&T Bell Labs Record,* August 1984.

Bemer, R. W., "A View of the History of the ISO Character Code." *Honeywell Computer Journal,* 1972.

Bloom, Murray Teigh, "Communication: Fast and Accurate." *American Business,* November 1956.

Boraiko, Allen A., "Harnessing Light by a Thread." *National Geographic,* October 1979.

Cieply, Michael, "When Hollywood Calls, It Will Likely Be from the Driver's Seat of a Cruising Car." *The Wall Street Journal,* May 30, 1986.

Clarke, Arthur C., "Extra-Terrestrial Relays." *Wireless World,* October 1945.

Cullers, D. K., Ivan R. Linscott, and Bernard M. Oliver, "Signal Processing in Seti." *Communications of the ACM,* November 1985.

"Data Transmission and the Real-Time Systems." *Dun's Review,* September 1965.

Derfler, Frank J., Jr., "Zero-Slot LANs: A Low-Cost Solution." *PC Magazine,* November 26, 1985.

Epstein, Nadine, "*Et Voila! Le Minitel.*" *The New York Times Magazine,* March 9, 1986.

Freese, Arthur S., "Microwaves." *Science Digest,* June 1970.

Gannes, Stuart, "New Medium for Messages." *Discover,* May 1984.

"Goeken Tunes Up His Microwave Net." *Business Week,* October 16, 1971.

Gunderson, Les C., and Donald B. Keck, "Optical Fibers: Where Light Outperforms Electrons." *Technology Review,* May-June, 1983.

Harrington, John V., "Radar Data Transmission." *Annals of the History of Computing,* October 1983.

Jastrow, Robert, "The Global Telecommunications Revolution." *Science Digest,* March 1984.

Jussawalla, Meheroo, "The Economic Implications of Satellite Technology and the Industrialization of Space." *Telecommunications Policy,* September 1984.

Kahn, Robert E., ed., "Scanning the Issue: Special Issue on Packet

Communications Networks." *Proceedings of the IEEE,* November 1978.

"Keeping Up with the Speed of Light." *The Economist,* January 25, 1986.

Kemeny, John G., and Thomas E. Kurtz, "Dartmouth Time-Sharing." *Science,* October 1968.

Kinsley, Carl, "High-Speed Printing Telegraph System." *Scientific American Supplement,* August 7, 1915.

Lamb, John, and Paul Tate, "British VAN Plan." *Datamation,* July 1, 1984.

Lewis, Richard, "Satellite Earth Stations." *PC World,* May 1986.

Loveday, Evelyn, "George Stibitz and the Bell Labs Relay Computers." *Datamation,* September 1977.

Mace, Scott, "Satellite-to-Micro Link." *Infoworld,* August 19, 1985.

Metcalfe, Robert M., and David R. Boggs, "Ethernet: Distributed Packet Switching for Local Computer Networks." *Communications of the ACM,* July 1976.

"The Murray Automatic Page-Printing Telegraph." *Scientific American,* September 8, 1906.

"Optical Fibers Straddle the Globe." *The Economist,* March 22, 1986.

Ornstein, S. M., et al., "The Terminal IMP for the ARPA Computer Network." *AFIPS Conference Proceedings.* 1972.

"A Perspective on SAGE: Discussion." *Annals of the History of Computing,* October 1983.

Pierce, John R., "The Transmission of Computer Data." *Scientific American,* September 1966.

Roberts, Lawrence G., "Computer Report III: Data by the Packet." *IEEE Spectrum,* February 1974.

Roberts, Lawrence G., and Barry D. Wessler, "Computer Network Development to Achieve Resource Sharing." *Proceedings, American Federation Information Processing Society,* Spring Joint Conference, 1970.

Rohwer, Jim, "The World on the Line." *The Economist,*

November 23, 1985.

"The Round AT&T Lost." *Business Week,* September 6, 1969.

"SABRE — Realtime Benchmark Has the Winning Ticket." *Data Management,* September 1981.

"Satellite Communications Firms Prepare for Growth in Small Earth Stations." *Aviation Week & Space Technology,* March 10, 1986.

Shuford, Richard C., "An Introduction to Fiber Optics." Parts 1 and 2. *BYTE,* December 1984 and January 1985.

Stibitz, George R., "The Relay Computers at Bell Labs." *Datamation,* April 1967.

"Telstar's Triumph." *Time,* July 20, 1962.

Valley, George E., Jr., "How the SAGE Development Began." *Annals of the History of Computing,* July 1985.

Voelcker, John, "Helping Computers Communicate." *IEEE Spectrum,* March 1986.

Wienski, Robert M., and H. Charles Baker, "Getting Ready for ISDN." *Business Communications Review,* November-December 1985.

Witt, Michael, "An Introduction to Layered Protocols." *BYTE,* September 1983.

Other Publications

Fiber Optics. Los Angeles, Calif.: Creative Strategies International, November 1981.

GTE Spacenet, *Technical Characteristics of GSTAR Satellites.* McLean, Va.: GTE Spacenet Corp., 1985.

GTE Telenet, *Packet Switching Principles, TD150.* Reston, Va.: GTE Telenet Communications Corp., 1985.

Link: Viewdata/Videotex Report, December 1985.

Roberts, Lawrence G., "The ARPANET & Computer Networks." Speech given at the ACM Conference on the History of Personal Workstations. January 9-10, 1986.

"Teletype-Computer Connection Simplified." *Stanford Research Institute Journal,* June 1967.

Acknowledgments

The index for this book was prepared by Mel Ingber. The editors also wish to thank the following individuals and institutions for their help in the preparation of this volume: **In Switzerland:** Geneva — Paul Kalezic, The International Telecommunication Union. **In the United States:** California — Los Angeles: Keith Uncapher, University of Southern California at Los Angeles; Menlo Park: John Van Geen, SRI International; Pasadena: John R. Pierce, California Institute of Technology; San Mateo: Lawrence Roberts, Net Express West, Inc.; Connecticut — Shelton: Charles Kao, ITT-ATC; District of Columbia — Gary P. Tobin, MCI; Lilliane Volcy, Federal Communications Commission; Maryland — Clarksburg: Fred Kelly, Comsat; Gaithersburg: Robert Rosenthal, National Bureau of Standards; Massachusetts — Berlington: Lasertron, Inc.; New Jersey — Basking Ridge: John R. Galanti, Bell Atlantic Mobile Systems; Bedminster: Perry Youngblood, American Telegraph & Telephone; New York — Corning: Alan R. Minthorn, Corning Glass Works; Poughkeepsie: John R. Knight, IBM Corporation; Texas — Richardson: David Horton, Amdahl Computers; Virginia — Alexandria: Derek Westervelt Kelly; McLean: Frederick E. Cramer, GTE Spacenet Corporation; Reston: Stuart Mathison and Philip M. Walker, GTE Telenet Inc.

Picture Credits

Credits from left to right are separated by semicolons; from top to bottom by dashes.
Cover, 6: Art by Peter A. Sawyer from Design Innovations, Inc. 10-17: Art by Steven R. Wagner from Moonlight Studios. 22, 23: Art by Peter A. Sawyer from Design Innovations, Inc.; art by John Drummond (2). 24, 25: Art by Peter A. Sawyer from Design Innovations, Inc. 29-37: Art by Matt McMullen. 38-45: Art by Peter A. Sawyer from Design Innovations, Inc. 50: Art by Tyrone Huntley. 51: Art by Tyrone Huntley except pins by John Drummond. 52, 53: Art by Tyrone Huntley. 58-61: Art by Wayne Vincent. 65-77: Art by Steven R. Wagner from Moonlight Studios. 78-93: Art by Peter A. Sawyer from Design Innovations, Inc. 98, 99: AT&T Bell Laboratories, art by Peter A. Sawyer from Design Innovations, Inc. 105-121: Art by William J. Hennessy Jr.

Index

Library of Congress Cataloguing in Publication Data
Communications
    (Understanding computers)
    Bibliography: p.
    Includes index
    1. Data transmission systems — Popular works.
2. Computer networks — Popular works.
I. Time-Life Books.   II. Series.
TK5105.C635 1986   384.3   86-14537
ISBN 0-8094-5700-8
ISBN 0-8094-5701-6 (lib. bdg.)

For information about any Time-Life book, please write:
Reader Information
Time-Life Books
541 North Fairbanks Court
Chicago, Illinois 60611

UNDERSTANDING COMPUTERS

GENERAL CONSULTANT

EUGENE F. O'NEILL, an engineer with the Bell Telephone Laboratories from 1941 to 1983, is editor and co-
author of *A History of Engineering and Science in the Bell
System: Transmission Technology 1925-1975* (AT&T,
1986). While at Bell Labs, he was Director of Telstar satellite projects and Executive Director of the transmission
division. In 1971 he received the IEEE Award in International Communications.

CONSULTANTS

GWEN BELL is the President of the Computer Museum in
Boston, Massachusetts.

ISABEL LIDA NIRENBERG has dealt with a wide range of
computer applications, from analysis of data collected by
the Pioneer space probes to the matching of children and
families for adoption agencies. She works at the Computer Center at the State University of New York at Albany.

WILLIAM STALLINGS is President of Comp/Comm Con-
sulting of Great Falls, Virginia, and lectures frequently.
Author of *Data and Computer Communications* (Macmillan, 1985), he holds a Ph.D. in computer science from the
Massachusetts Institute of Technology.